West Academic Publishing's Law School Advisory Board

Federal Income Taxation

Second Edition

Joel S. Newman
Professor Emeritus
Wake Forest University School of Law

A SHORT & HAPPY GUIDE® SERIES

WEST
ACADEMIC
PUBLISHING

a short & happy guide series is a trademark registered in the U.S. Patent and Trademark Office.

© 2017 LEG, Inc. d/b/a West Academic
© 2019 LEG, Inc. d/b/a West Academic
    444 Cedar Street, Suite 700
    St. Paul, MN 55101
    1-877-888-1330
Printed in the United States of America

ISBN: 978-1-64242-690-8

Preface

I'm relatively short and I'm relatively happy. And I teach tax. So, it seems like a pretty good fit.

JOEL NEWMAN

December 2018

Table of Contents

A Short & Happy Guide to Federal Income Taxation

Second Edition

CHAPTER I

Introduction

A. A Little Angst?

So you signed up for the basic tax course and now you're having second thoughts. You know that you really should start reading the first assignment in the casebook, but you just can't get yourself to do it. So you buy this book instead, and crack it open. Well, at least that's something.

B. Why Tax Is Important

1. For Everyone

Tax law is really important. It even changes the way the world looks, in ways that you might not have imagined. Have a look at this photo of one of the older sections of Southampton, England.

Why are the windows bricked up? Well, back in the day, the city fathers of London were looking for a way to tax rich people. They reasoned that only rich people had glass windows, so they taxed glass windows. In response, many of the rich people of London bricked up their glass windows, and decided to do their conspicuous consumption some other way. And the windows are still bricked up today.

Have a look at this photo of lovely canal houses in Amsterdam.

See how narrow the houses are? The houses and the interior stairways are so narrow that it would be impossible to move furniture up the stairs. So how do you furnish the third floor?

See the hooks that stick out from the tops of the gables? Perhaps you can see it better in this close-up.

You throw a rope over those hooks. Then, you haul the furniture up the outside of the house, and swing it in through the window.

Why are the houses so narrow? Well, back in the day, the city fathers of Amsterdam were looking for a way to tax rich people. They reasoned that only rich people would have wide houses, so they taxed wide houses. In response, many of the rich people built narrow houses instead, complete with the hooks coming out of the gables.

Here's a "salt box" house.

How come it has two stories in the front and only one in the back?

Well, back in the day, the taxing authorities figured that folks who lived in two-story houses were richer than folks who lived in one-story houses. So they levied a special tax on two-story houses. But the tax only applied if the second story went all the way back. In response, a lot of rich people built houses with two stories in front and only one in the back. With its steeply sloping roof, the house looks like a wooden salt box, popular in colonial New England. Many of those houses are still standing.

Here's a cute dog.

Why is its tail so short? Well, back in the day, in eighteenth-century England, there was a tax on working dogs. Working dogs were distinguishable by their long tails. In response, the English people shortened their dogs' tails, so that they wouldn't be taken for taxable, working dogs. And the fashion stuck.

The world is a very different place from what it might have been, because of tax law. Even the way it looks.

2. For You

Tax lawyers aren't the only ones who need to know something about tax law; all lawyers do. Tax affects everything. Whatever your area of practice, there will be tax consequences you need to know about. If you're a litigator, you'll need to know if the damage awards your plaintiff clients win are taxable, and if the damages your defendant clients pay are deductible. If you do divorce work, your clients will be intensely interested in the tax aspects of alimony payments. And so it goes.

C. Why Taxes?

In 2017, the federal government spent around 4 trillion dollars. Where did it come up with the money? It could have printed it, or it could have borrowed it. Actually, the federal government does print money every year, and it does borrow money every year. But it would be a bad idea to fund the entire $4 trillion by printing and borrowing money. Why? Because both cause inflation. If you keep the national supply of goods and services constant, and print more money, then you'll have more dollars chasing the same goods and services. Therefore, the price of everything will go up. That's inflation.

Similarly, if the government borrows a lot of money, then interest rates will go up. When interest rates go up, the cost of everything goes up. Again, that's inflation.

It's not that inflation is so awful. It's just that inflation burdens some people—say, retired folks on a fixed income, more than other people—say, hedge fund managers. Most people would not want to distribute the burdens in quite that way. If we are not going to fund the entire federal government by printing money and borrowing money, then we have to come up with something else. That something else is tax.

D. Why Tax Income?

Let's say we had decided to fund the entire $4 trillion through taxation. The population of the United States was around 325 million people that year. Why didn't we just divide the people into the money? If every man, woman and child in the United States would just have ponied up around $12,300, we'd have had the $4 trillion we need. Simple. That's called a head tax.

Actually, for our purposes, that $4 trillion figure was a mite high. As mentioned before, we do borrow money, and we do print money, so we didn't need to generate the entire $4 trillion through taxation. Total direct federal revenue was only about $3.3 trillion, of which a little under $1.6 trillion came from the federal income tax. 1.6 trillion divided by 325 million people is just under $5,000 per person. Now that's better, isn't it?

There's just one problem. Quite a few of us couldn't have afforded $5,000 that year. Babies, for example. Actually, most children. On top of that, quite a few adults in the US are barely making ends meet, and just can't come up with $5,000 to fund the federal government. You know what makes it worse? This year, the feds are going to spend another $4 trillion, if not more. So they'll want each and every one of us to fork over another $5,000 next year, and the year after that, and the year after that.

On the other hand, there are quite a few other folks in the US who can afford to pay a lot more than $5,000 per year. So what should we do? We should levy taxes based upon ability to pay. Those of us who are able to pay more to fund government expenditures should do so. Those of us, like infants and low income people, who are able to pay less, should pay less, or even nothing at all. In fact, even though there were 325 million people in the United States in 2017, only about 140 million tax returns were filed.

How do you measure ability to pay? You can't. At least, you can't do it directly. You can try to tax windows, or front footage, or multistory houses, or working dogs. You see how well that worked. Or, you can go after broader, measurable attributes, which, you hope, will give you a reasonably good idea of what ability to pay really is. Pretty much everyone agrees that the three best measurable attributes are income, spending, and wealth.

As a matter of fact, neither income, nor spending, nor wealth can alone give an adequate measurement of ability to pay taxes. The best thing is to use all three. And that is what we do. It's just that the same level of government doesn't necessarily do all three. Here in the United States, generally speaking, the federal government predominantly taxes income, the states tax income and spending (in the form of sales taxes), and the local governments tax wealth, in the form of property taxes. That's the big picture. There are exceptions. Some local governments tax income as well, and the federal government taxes wealth, at least in the form of the Estate and Gift taxes, which tax transfers of wealth. But the big picture is pretty much as I have stated it.

Other countries have made different choices. While our national government predominantly taxes income, European national governments predominantly tax spending, in the form of Value Added Taxes. You might, in your many hours of leisure, want to muse on which is the better choice. However, for the purpose of this book, and the course you are taking, we accept that the federal government has chosen income. Now, we just have to figure out how that income tax works.

E. A Little Policy: Progressivity and Regressivity

Recently, there has been a lot of talk about income inequality. The rich are getting richer, the poor are getting poorer, and the gap between rich and poor is growing. Taxes can play a part in reducing economic inequality. If taxes take more money from rich people and less money from poor people, and then those tax revenues are redistributed in favor of the poor, then that is a step toward alleviating inequality. How do we do that? Through progressive rates.

Let's define some terms. A **flat**, or **proportional**, rate structure is one in which all income is taxed at the same, flat rate. For example, if the rate were 20%, then the tax on $1.00 of income would be $.20. The tax on $100.00 would be $20.00, and the tax on $100,000,000 would be $20,000,000. Note that, as income goes up, the amount of tax paid goes up, but the rate of taxation does not. Here's a flat tax.

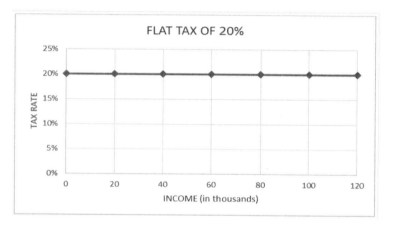

A progressive rate structure is one in which the rate goes up as the income goes up. However, it is the marginal rate—the rate of tax on the last dollar of income—that goes up. Imagine, for example, a tax system in which income from $0 to $10,000 is taxed at 10%, and income in excess of $10,000 is taxed at 20%. Suppose that a taxpayer had income of $18,000. Such a taxpayer would pay 10% tax on her first $10,000 of income, and 20% tax on the remaining $8,000 of income. The total tax would be:

First $10,000	x	10%	=	$1,000
+ Final $8,000	x	20%	=	$1,600
		Total tax		$2,600

The **marginal** tax rate is the rate of tax on the last, marginal, dollar of income. Here is a graph of the marginal rates of the tax described above.

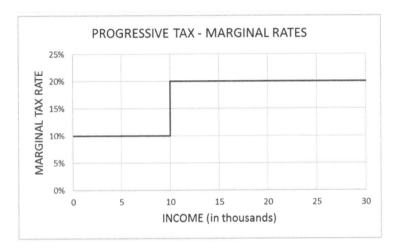

The **effective** tax rate is computed by dividing the tax by the income. Thus, in the tax above, the effective tax rate for $10,000 of income is:

$$\frac{\text{Tax}}{\text{Income}} \quad \frac{\$1,000}{\$10,000} \quad = \quad 10\%$$

The effective tax rate for $18,000 of income is:

$$\frac{\text{Tax}}{\text{Income}} \quad \frac{\$2,600}{\$18,000} \quad = \quad 14.4\%$$

Here is a graph of the effective tax rates of the tax described above. The graph of the effective tax rates of a progressive tax will always have a positive slope.

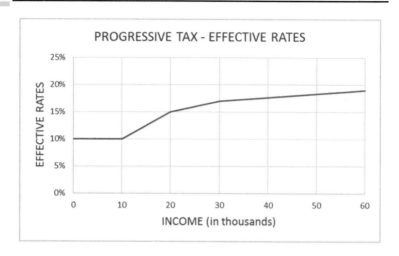

A **regressive** tax structure is one in which the rate goes down as the income goes up. If the first $10,000 were taxed at 20%, and all income in excess of $10,000 were taxed at 10%, the graph of marginal tax rates would look like this:

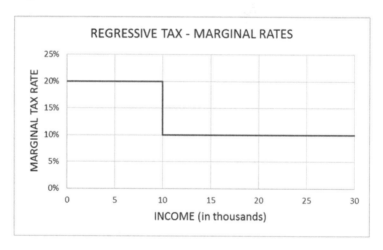

A graph of the effective tax rates of a regressive tax will always have a negative slope.

Pretty much everyone agrees that a flat or proportional tax structure is okay. Some people, especially those concerned with income inequality, think that a progressive rate structure is preferable. Nobody likes a regressive tax structure.

F. A Final Tip

You don't want to tick off your tax teacher. At least, not unintentionally. So, let's get the case names right. In the early years, tax case titles referred to the name of the Commissioner at the time the case was brought. In Welch v. Helvering, 290 U.S. 111 (1933), for example, Welch was the taxpayer; Helvering was the Commissioner of Internal Revenue. There may have been only one federal tax case involving Welch, but there were quite a few involving Helvering. We finally realized that using the actual commissioners' names was confusing. More modern cases simply refer to the Commissioner, as in Commissioner v. Duberstein.

So, if your instructor asks you in class to name the early case which provides the authority for something or other, don't say, "Oh, that's the Helvering case." That would probably tick her off. Use the other guy to name the case.

Just so you know, here are the names and dates of a few of the early Commissioners:

Robert H. Lucas	1929-1930
David Burnet	1930-1933
Guy T. Helvering	1933-1943

Enough said?

CHAPTER II

A Stroll Through a Tax Return

Generally speaking, lawyers don't fill out tax returns. Accountants do. Tax returns, however, are how most taxpayers think about our tax law. Tax returns, and their accompanying Instructions, are the predominant way that the government explains the tax law to the taxpayers. So, with due reluctance, I present a tax return.

A. The Facts

Let's say you're single. You earned $25,000 in wages last year. Your employer withheld a total of $2,500 from your salary. Here's your tax return—somewhat edited:

2018 1040 Income Tax Return		
1.	Wages, Salaries and Tips	$25,000
* * *		
6.	Total Income	$25,000
7.	Adjusted Gross Income	$25,000

		[If you have no adjustments to income, enter the amount from Line 6]	
8.		Standard Deduction or Itemized Deduction [Single or married filing separately, $12,000]	$12,000
✱ ✱ ✱			
10.		Taxable Income [subtract Line 8 from Line 7]	$13,000
11.		Tax [from tables in Instructions] [subtract any credits]	$1,370
✱ ✱ ✱			
15.		Total Tax	$1,370
16.		Federal income tax withheld	$2,500
✱ ✱ ✱			
18.		Total Payments	$2,500
Refund			
19.		If Line 18 is more than Line 15, this is the amount you overpaid	$1,130
20.		Amount of Line 19 you want refunded to you	$1,130
✱ ✱ ✱			
21.		Amount of Line 19 you want applied to your 2019 estimated tax	0

Now let's see what you did. You put your $25,000 wages on Line 1, and again on Line 6. You subtracted $12,000 because Line 8 told you to. That leaves you with $13,000 taxable income, which you enter on Line 10. Your tax, according to the tables in the Instructions [not provided] is $1,370, which you enter on Line 15.

Your employer withheld $2,500 from your salary, so you enter that on Lines 16 and 189.

When you subtract your Total Payments of $2,500 [Line 18] from your Total Tax of $1,370 [Line 15], it turns out that the Feds owe you a refund of $1,130, which you happily enter on Lines 19 and 20.

So, you **add** your income. That gets you to Line 6. You **subtract** your deductions. That gets you to Taxable Income on Line 10. By going to the Tax Tables, you **apply the tax rates**. That gets you to the Total Tax on Line 15. Finally, you **subtract** your payments and credits. That gets you to your $1,130 refund on Lines 19 and 20. Adding is okay; subtraction can be really fun.

B. Deductions vs. Credits

Notice that you subtracted twice.[*] The first time was on Line 10, *before* you went to the Tax Tables. The second time was on Line 19, *after* you went to the Tax Tables. When you subtracted *before* the Tax Tables, those were *deductions*. When you subtracted *after*, those were *payments and credits*.

One dollar of deduction will not reduce your tax bill by a dollar. Rather, it will reduce your tax bill by one dollar times your tax bracket. For example, if you are in the 25% tax bracket, which means that your last dollar of taxable income is taxed at the rate of 25%, then one dollar of deduction will save you not one dollar, but 25¢. One dollar of payment or credit, on the other hand, will reduce your tax bill by one dollar.

Let's see why that is true. Imagine a tax system in which all income is taxed at 10%. You have $101 dollars of taxable income. What is your tax on the $101? What would your tax be if you were allowed to deduct $1 from that $101? What would your tax be if you

---

[*] You would have subtracted a third time if you had Adjustments to Income, when you went from Line 6 to Line 7. But you didn't. The Business Deductions described in Chapter V would be Adjustments to Income.

were allowed a credit of $1 from the taxes on your $101 of taxable income?

Your tax on $101.00, at 10%, is $10.10.

What if you were allowed to deduct $1? Then your taxable income would be $100. Your tax would be 10% of $100.00, or $10.00

Compare the $10.10 you paid *before* the deduction to the $10.00 tax paid *after* the deduction. That one dollar deduction saved you 10¢ in taxes. That's the amount of the deduction, multiplied by your tax rate.

What if, instead of a $1 deduction, you were allowed a $1 credit?

Start with you tax on $101.00. Again, that is 10% of $101.00, or $10.10. Now, subtract the $1.00 credit from the taxes owed.

Taxes before credit	$10.10
– Credit	$1.00
Taxes after credit	$9.10

The one dollar *credit* reduced your tax bill by one dollar. However, the one dollar *deduction* reduced your tax bill by ten cents. That's because the credit is subtracted *after* you apply the rates, while the deduction is applied *before*.

Keep this in mind, when considering which items are deductible, and which are creditable.

CHAPTER III

What Is Income?

A. Definition

We managed to get this far without cracking open the Internal Revenue Code. But alas, the time has come.

Even those of us who like tax would agree that the Internal Revenue Code is often annoying. The Code and Regulations are pretty long. So, would you rather read the entire Code and Regulations, or would you rather read WAR AND PEACE three times? At least, WAR AND PEACE has a plot. But here's the thing. You don't have to read the Code and Regulations cover to cover. Nobody does that. You just need to know your way around it. Then, you need to read the specific provisions relevant to your inquiry. And here's another thing. No one will pay you to read WAR AND PEACE. Not even once.

Here goes. Section 61 of the Internal Revenue Code provides:

> Except as otherwise provided in this subtitle, gross income means all income from whatever source derived, including (but not limited to) the following items:

Then it goes on to list fifteen things.

How annoying is that? For starters, it says, essentially, that "income is income." I mean, what if you asked me to define "automobile," and I said, "An automobile is an automobile." That is not terribly helpful.

Also, it starts with "Except as otherwise provided. . ." That tells you that, whatever gross income might be, (and so far, they're not exactly telling you, are they?) you will also have to consider exceptions to gross income, which you will find somewhere else in the statute. Bummer.

Let's talk about those fifteen listed items. Notice that the 15 items are prefaced by ". . .including (but not limited to)." That tells you that the fifteen items are a non-exclusive list. If you find something in the list, like, say rents, in Section 61(a)(5), then you know that rent is income. But other, nonlisted items can also be income.

What if you're walking down the street, and you find a $100 bill, which you pick up. That's known as "windfall income." Windfall isn't one of the fifteen listed items. Does that mean that it isn't taxable income? Not necessarily. Remember, the fifteen items are a non-exclusive list. Windfall income is taxable income, but you have to go to the cases to find out.

The Supreme Court, in Glenshaw Glass v. Commissioner, 348 U.S. 426 (1955), described income this way:

> Here we have instances of undeniable accessions to wealth, clearly realized, and over which the taxpayers have complete dominion.

Now, that's better—a little. At least, it answers some questions. What if you borrow $100. Do you have $100 income? No. You don't have "complete dominion" over the $100, because you'll have to give it back. Also, income has to be "clearly realized." **"Realization"** means something. Stay tuned.

B. Sales Proceeds

Say you bought a widget on January 2 for $100,000, and by December 31 of that year, the value had gone up to $105,000. Lucky you.

Suppose you sell your widget in December for $105,000. You have taxable income, but how much? Section 1001 says that your [taxable] gain is the excess of your amount realized over your adjusted basis. Amount realized is defined in Section 1001(b). Basis is defined in Section 1012, and adjustments to basis are described in Section 1016.

In this simple example, your amount realized is the sales proceeds of $105,000, and your basis is what you paid for the widget, or $100,000. The excess is computed as follows:

Amount realized	$105,000
- Basis	$100,000
Excess	$5,000

So your taxable gain is $5,000.

What about inflation? What if everything in the universe that was worth $100,000 in January is now worth $105,000? It's not as if the value of your widget really went up. Rather, the purchasing power of the dollar went down. Does that mean you don't have taxable income? No, it does not. As it turns out, it's just too difficult to adjust for inflation. The good news is that, when you pay your taxes on the $5,000 gain, you'll be paying in cheaper dollars.

What if you don't sell your widget? You just sit around looking smug. However, you are still $5,000 better off in December than you were last January. Does the tax code recognize that $5,000 as taxable income? No, it does not. That's where **realization** comes in.

You don't recognize taxable income until you sell the widget. You might not sell that widget for years. In fact, you might never sell it.

That isn't fair. If you put your money in the savings bank, it will earn interest. That interest is specifically mentioned in Section 61(a)(4). It will be taxed to you as soon as it is posted to your account, even if you don't withdraw it. However if, instead of putting your money in the bank, you buy a widget, any increase in the value of that widget will not be taxed to you, unless or until you sell it. Why is it that you're taxed on the interest immediately, but you're not taxed on the appreciation in value of your widget until you sell it?

There are two good reasons why we don't tax unrealized income. The first one is valuation. Remember that I told you that you bought the widget for $100,000, and that by December it was worth $105,000. Well, why should you believe me? How do you know that the widget was really worth $105,000 in December? You could appraise it. Do you really want to appraise every single asset in the country every year, to see if its value has changed?

If you waited for a realization event, this valuation problem would go away. Remember—the classic realization event is a sale. When there is a sale between an arm's length buyer and an arm's length seller, it is presumed that the sale price reflects the fair market value of the sold asset. Goodbye valuation problem.

The second reason is liquidity. Let's say that you bought a house—not a widget—for $100,000 in January of Year 1, and that it went up in value to $105,000 by December of Year 1. Let's say that the IRS taxed your $5,000 unrealized appreciation at 10%. Now you owe $500. Where are you going to get it? Let's say that you have no other liquid assets, so you have to sell your house in order to have the cash with which to pay the tax. Now you have

Sales proceeds	$105,000
– Tax payment	$500
Net cash	$104,500

However, you have no place to live. So you buy another house, for $104,500. Your new house won't be quite as nice as the one you just sold. The house you just sold was worth $105,000, but you only spent $104,500 on its replacement.

Let's say that, during Year 2, your new house goes up another $5,000 in value, to $109,500. So, you owe 10% tax, or $500, on the $5,000 of unrealized appreciation in Year 2. But where will you get the $500? Again, you sell the house. Now you have net cash of

Sales proceeds	$109,500
– Tax payment	$500
Net cash	$109,000

But again, you have no house. So you buy another house. However, it won't be quite as nice as House #2. Keep this up, and you'll end up living in a cardboard box.

The liquidity problem is solved if we wait for the realization event. Realization happens when you choose to sell your house. When you do, you will be able to use the cash sales proceeds to pay the tax. Thus, the realization requirement eliminates the liquidity problem.

You probably noticed that basis is really important. Basis is also really good, because you get to subtract it from amount realized. Here are a few things you need to know about basis:

- Basis represents historical cost. Say you bought a widget for $100 in Year 1. In Year 2, it went up in value to $250. In Year 3, its value dropped to $15. It doesn't matter. Your basis remains what you paid for it in Year 1—$100.

- Basis is not adjusted for inflation. Maybe it should be, but it isn't. When inflation goes up, the value of a dollar goes down. Arguably, if you sell your widget in Year 5 for $150, it makes no sense to subtract 100 Year 1 dollars from 150 Year 5 dollars, because Year 1 dollars and Year 5 dollars are not the same thing. They are like apples and oranges. But it doesn't matter; that's what we do.

- Basis represents your original investment in the property, plus any further investments, which you used to improve the property. It doesn't matter if you overpaid. It doesn't matter if your "improvements" didn't actually improve anything. Your basis is your investment—smart or stupid.

- It doesn't matter where you got the money that you invested. Wherever it came from, that's your basis. The money could have been taxable to you, or taxfree. It could have been earned as salary, or even stolen. It could even be borrowed money. That's right—you could borrow *someone else's money* to buy the widget, and it's still part of *your* basis. More on that later.

Now, here are a few thoughts about amount realized. According to § 1001(b), Amount realized is "the sum of any money received plus the fair market value of the property (other than money) received." That means:

- If I sell my widget for $100 cash, my amount realized is $100.

- If I trade my widget for a thingamajig worth $100, my amount realized is still $100. The thingqamajig is ". . .property (other than money) received."

- If I sell my widget for $50 cash plus a thingamajig worth $50, my amount realized is still $100.

- If I sell my widget in return for your repayment of my $100 pre-existing debt, my amount realized is still $100. More on that later.

We have discussed basis and amount realized. You know that the important calculation is

Amount realized

– Basis
_____

Gain/loss

So far, all we talked about is gains. What if Basis is greater than Amount Realized, and you have a loss? What's the tax consequence of that?

It depends. Here's the big "Heads we win; tails you lose" of tax law: All recognized gains are taxable. Not all recognized losses are deductible. Business losses are deductible; personal losses, generally speaking, are not. This is a crucial point. I'll remind you about it a few more times over the course of this book.

C. Other Aspects of Income

1. Should Illegal Income Be Taxable?

Hell, yes. Do you really think that criminals should earn their income taxfree while the rest of us have to pay taxes?

For a while, there was some doubt about this issue, for two reasons. First, stolen money (to take one example) seems a lot like borrowed money. Remember—the Supreme Court in *Glenshaw Glass* said that you don't have taxable income unless you have complete dominion over it. So, you don't have taxable income when you borrow money, because you have to pay it back. Similarly, many argued that you don't have taxable income when you steal money, because, again, theoretically, you have to pay it back. In fact, for a while, this concept led to a distinction between extorted money, when the victim knew you took the money, and, in effect, consented to the taking, and stolen money, where the victim may not have known, and certainly didn't consent. Based upon this distinction, extorted money was income, and stolen money was not.

The other reason was that it appeared a bit unseemly to tax illegal income. It does, in a way, make the government appear to be a partner in crime. Ironically, this argument was most famously made by Judge Martin Manton, who was later himself convicted of accepting bribes.

Now, both of these reasons have been rejected, and the Supreme Court has made it crystal clear that all income—legal and illegal—is taxable. So, if illegal income is taxable, then are the expenses incurred in generating that income deductible? Most of the time, the answer is yes. But that's a deduction thing. Stay tuned.

2. *Imputed Income*

Suppose I'm a house painter. I paint a house, and charge $500. That's taxable income. What if I paint my own house? Shouldn't that generate taxable income of $500 to me as well?

Suppose that I own rental property. I rent it out to a third party for $500. That rent is taxable income to me. What if I live in the property myself? Shouldn't that also generate taxable income of $500 to me?

Imputed income is the income you generate when you perform services for yourself—like the painter, or when you use your own property—like the homeowner. Some countries tax some types of imputed income; we do not. Taxing imputed income would be problematic, for valuation and liquidity reasons, among others. Yet, failure to tax imputed income leads to unfairness. Bank savings accounts and houses are both income-producing properties. Why should I be taxed on the interest from my bank savings account, but not on the rental value of my house?

3. *Expectations*

Suppose I've been watching too much HGTV, and I decide to flip a house. I buy a dilapidated house at a foreclosure sale for $50,000, and I spend $75,000 sprucing it up. I fully expect to sell it for $175,000. That would be a nice $50,000 profit. But, as it turns out, nobody likes my renovated house as much as I do, and I can only sell it for $125,000. That's exactly what I put into it; I make no profit at all.

I expected to make $50,000. I actually made zero. Do I have a loss? No. Gain or loss is determined by subtracting basis from Amount Realized. In this case, the computation is

Amount realized	$125,000
- Basis	$125,000
Gain/loss	$0

Gain or loss reflects what actually happened, not what you thought would happen.

4. *Income to Your Benefit*

Suppose that I agree to paint my neighbor's house for $1,000. I finish the job, and my neighbor is satisfied. He comes to my door with one thousand dollars cash in his hand, ready to pay. I tell him to give the money to my local grocery store instead. The grocery store duly accepts the money in prepayment of the next $1,000 of groceries that I buy. Have I shifted the taxable income of the $1,000 from me to the grocery store? No. I am still taxable on the $1,000 of compensation income. I earned it. Further, even if it was not paid directly to me, it was paid at my direction, and to my benefit.

Imagine two scenarios. In the first, my neighbor pays me the $1,000 for painting his house. Then I use the money to buy $1,000 worth of groceries. In the second, my neighbor, in exchange for my painting his house, pays the $1,000 directly to the grocery store, on my account.

In both scenarios, I paint my neighbor's house, and end up with $1,000 worth of groceries. My neighbor is out $1,000 cash, but ends up with a freshly painted house. Scenarios that have the same outcome should be taxed the same. Therefore, if, in scenario #1, I have $1,000 taxable income, then I should also have $1,000 taxable income in scenario #2. And I do.

What if I had previously borrowed $1,000 from the bank? Imagine that, when my neighbor shows up to pay me for painting his house, I direct him to use the money to pay off my loan at the bank. Same result. I have $1,000 taxable income.

What if I had previously borrowed $1,000 from my neighbor? Suppose that, when he shows up to pay me for painting his house, I simply tell him to keep the money, and consider my debt repaid. Same result. My neighbor is making a payment (to himself) at my direction, and to my benefit. So, it's taxable income to me.

These last few examples, however, suggest a deeper look at borrowing and repaying money.

5. Debt

a. Borrowing and Repaying

We already know, from *Glenshaw Glass*, that loan proceeds are not income. But let's take a closer look.

Say I borrow $1,000. Am I better off? No.

Have a look at my balance sheet, before and after. Remember: assets minus liabilities equal net worth.

Before

Assets	Liabilities
$0	$0
	Net Worth
	$0

After

Assets	Liabilities
$1,000	$1,000
	Net Worth
	$0

Before I borrowed the money, my Net Worth was zero. After I borrowed the money, my net worth is still zero. Borrowing $1,000 increases my assets, because I now have $1,000 cash in loan proceeds, which I didn't have before. That's the good news. The bad news is that I have also increased my liabilities by $1,000. Yes, I have $1,000, but I can't keep it forever. Some day, I'll have to pay it back. Borrowing the $1,000 effects no change in my net worth; I have no taxable income.

Now, what happens when I pay it back? Here's my balance sheet while I owe the money:

Before

Assets	Liabilities
$1,000	$1,000
	Net Worth
	$0

And here's my balance sheet when I pay it back:

After

Assets	Liabilities
$0	$0
	Net Worth
	$0

My net worth of zero is unchanged. Paying the money back does decrease my cash on hand, but it also wipes out my debt. So, just as borrowing the money, without more, doesn't change my net worth, paying it back, without more, doesn't change it either. Therefore, the repayment of a loan, without more, has no tax consequences, just like the borrowing of the money in the first place.

But what if your debt is discharged even if you don't pay it back? Say that, for whatever reason, my creditor decides to forgive the loan.

Now, looking at the balance sheet, something *has* happened. Here's your balance sheet before:

Before

Assets	Liabilities
$1,000	$1,000
	Net Worth
	$0

Here's your balance sheet after:

After

Assets	Liabilities
$1,000	$0
	Net Worth
	$1,000

Now, your net worth went up by $1,000. That should be taxable income, unless you can find some exception to prove that it isn't.

The balance sheet explanation is what the Supreme Court used in United States v. Kirby Lumber, Co., 284 U.S. 1 (1931), when it held that a discharge of debt is taxable income. That decision, and that logic, covers most cases, but not all. Here's a better one.

Why, when you borrowed the money in the first place, were you not taxed on the loan proceeds? Because you were expected to pay it back. Now, what happens if, for whatever reason, you don't have to pay them back? Then, those initial expectations turned out to be wrong. We thought you would pay back the loan, but you didn't. If we had known at the outset that you wouldn't pay back the loan, then we would have taxed you on the $1,000 when you received it. Well, it's too late for that. So, instead, we'll tax you now, on the discharge of debt.

Let's review. First, if I borrow $1000, and then pay it back myself, then the $1000 loan proceeds are not taxable to me, and the $1000 repayment has no tax effect. Note that there was no discharge of debt; I paid it back myself.

Second, if someone else paid it back, then it has to be taken into account, somehow. Suppose that I owe $1000. If my employer is about to pay me $1000 salary, and I tell him to pay the $1000 to my creditor, rather than to me, that $1000 is taxable salary income to me.

Suppose that I bought Blackacre for $1,100. I paid $100 cash, and took out a mortgage for the remaining $1,000. Taking out the mortgage is not a taxable event to me; that's just another form of borrowing money, and borrowing money is not a taxable event. Further, my basis in Blackacre is $1,100—the $100 cash, plus the $1,000 debt. That $1,000 mortgage debt is simply the source of the $1,000 that I invested in Blackacre [See b. Basis and Debt, below]. My investment in Blackacre should constitute my basis, no matter where I got the money.

Now let's say I sold Blackacre for $1,100. The Buyer gives me $100 cash, and uses another $1,000 to pay off the mortgage. My amount realized is $1,100. Since my basis is also $1,100, I have no gain, no loss. My amount realized includes the mortgage debt discharged. It doesn't matter if I actually, physically get to touch the $1,000 before I pay it over to the mortgage bank, or if the Buyer immediately pays the $1,000 to the mortgage bank to discharge the debt, or if the Buyer assumes the mortgage debt, paying it off over time. Either way, my amount realized includes the debt discharged of $1,000.

What if I owe the $1,000, but I can't pay it back? If my creditor forgives the debt, then I have taxable income from the discharge of indebtedness, under general income tax principles. There are, however, exceptions. If the debt was discharged in bankruptcy, it will be taxfree under § 108. Further, if my creditor was also, say, my father, then maybe the discharge of debt was actually a gift from him to me. In that case, it's tax free income to me, as you will see in the next chapter.

b. Basis and Debt

Let's say I bought a house for $100,000. Does it matter where the $100,000 came from? No, it does not. It doesn't matter whether you earned it as salary, stole it, or found it under a tree. It doesn't even matter whether you acquired the $100,000 in a taxable way, or in a nontaxable way. Still, it's the amount that you invested in the property, so it's your basis.

What if you got the $100,000 by borrowing it from someone else? Same thing. The source of the money is irrelevant. Borrowing is simply another source. Borrowed money used to acquire property will be part of the basis in that property.

What if you borrow the money from the seller? You go to the closing, you give the seller an IOU, and she gives you the title. Same thing. The borrowed money is part of your basis. It doesn't matter from whom you borrow it. It doesn't even matter when you borrowed it. Even if you borrow it from the seller, it is still part of your basis. Crane v. Commissioner, 331 U.S. 1 (1947), makes that clear.

This is really good news. Basis is good. First of all, when you sell, you subtract basis from amount realized. Therefore, the more basis you have, the more you can subtract, and the less taxable gain you have. Second, as you will find out later, depreciation deductions are good, and you can only take depreciation deductions if you have basis. You can create basis even if you don't use any of your own money. Now, there's bad news, but I'll let you enjoy the good news for a moment before we get to the bad news.

c. Debt and Amount Realized

Section 1001(b) says that Amount Realized is:

the sum of any money received plus the fair market value of the property (other than money) received.

We know that, if you sell your property for $105,000 cash, your Amount Realized is $105,000. What if you sold your property for $60,000 cash and a sports car worth $45,000? Your Amount Realized would be $105,000—the sum of the $60,000 cash and the $45,000 property. What if you sold your property for $60,000 cash paid to you, plus a payment of $45,000 to your bookie, to pay off your debts? Same thing. Your amount realized is $105,000. Discharged debt can be part of amount realized.

What if you bought the property without paying any cash? Instead, you gave an IOU for $100,000 to your Seller. Now, you sell the property to your Buyer, for a cash payment of $5,000 to you, plus a discharge of your $100,000 debt? Your amount realized is going to be $105,000 again—the sum of $5,000 cash paid to you, plus the noncash property received, in the form of the $100,000 discharge of your debt. What's more, it doesn't matter if your Buyer pays off your debt in cash at the closing, or merely assumes your debt, promising to pay it off over time. Either way, you're off the hook, and the $100,000 debt repayment is part of your amount realized.

That's the bad news I was warning you about. The good news is that debt can be a part of your basis. The bad news is that the discharge of that debt is part of your amount realized, too.

d.   *Tufts*

The holding of Commissioner v. Tufts, 461 U.S. 300 (1983), applies when property is subject to *nonrecourse debt*, and the *amount of the debt is greater than the fair market value of the collateral property*.

First, let's talk about *recourse* and *nonrecourse* debt. Say you borrow money, using Blackacre as collateral, and you default on the debt. What happens? It depends. If it was *nonrecourse* debt, then the creditor can only go after (have recourse to) the collateral—Blackacre. If the value of Blackacre was not sufficient to pay off the debt, then the creditor is out of luck. That is because the creditor has no further recourse. On the other hand, if it was *recourse* debt, then the creditor can not only go after the collateral, but, if necessary, the creditor can also go after you.

When does it make a difference? It makes no difference if the debt is less than the value of the collateral. Say, for example, that the debt was $100 and the value of the collateral was $400. If you default on the debt, then the creditor will take Blackacre, sell it, repay himself the $100 debt, and give you whatever remains. In this case, recourse vs. nonrecourse doesn't matter.

What if, however, the debt was $400 and the value of the collateral was $100? If you default on that debt, and it's *nonrecourse*, the creditor can take Blackacre and sell it for $100. After that, he is out of luck. However, if the debt was *recourse*, then the creditor can take Blackacre, sell it for $100, and then go after you for the remaining $300. As you can see, with *recourse* debt, creditors have a better chance of getting all of their money back. *Nonrecourse* debt is riskier to the creditor. They would charge higher interest to compensate for the risk. Usually, *nonrecourse* loans will not even be offered to some borrowers, such as personal homeowners.

Imagine that you had a *nonrecourse* loan for $400, with collateral worth only $100. How much do you really owe? Arguably, since the worst that the creditor can do to you is to take away your $100 of collateral, you don't owe more than $100. Paying off any more than $100 worth of debt in order to save collateral of $100 might be, I don't know— moral, but, in a sense, it would not be prudent.

You owe $400 on a *nonrecourse* loan, and the collateral, Blackacre, is worth only $100. Let's say that you abandon the property to the creditor, freeing yourself from the debt. That's a realization event, treated like a sale. Your amount realized is the debt discharged. You subtract your basis, and determine whether you have gain or loss.

What is your debt discharged, for purposes of computing amount realized? In *Commissioner v. Tufts*, the taxpayer argued that the debt was only $100, since, practically speaking, that was all he owed. Accordingly, he argued that the amount realized was only $100. The Supreme Court rejected that argument, holding that the amount realized was the face amount of the debt, or $400.

The Supreme Court majority opinion makes sense. No matter what the debt is now, you actually borrowed $400 when you took out the loan. You had the creditor's $400 to play with. Now, that is your debt. If you abandon the property to discharge the debt, your amount realized is $400.

The majority opinion in *Tufts* also held that there was one transaction—amount realized minus basis. Let's say that your adjusted basis in the property was $250. The one transaction would be:

Amount realized (debt discharged)	$400
– Basis	$250
Gain	$150

The concurring opinion saw two transactions. The Real Estate transaction looks like this:

Amount realized (fair market value of real estate)	$100
– Basis	$250
Loss	($150)

The Debt Transaction looks like this:

Amount borrowed	$400
– Amount repaid (through abandonment of RE to creditor)	$100
Discharge of debt income	$300

Note that the total income in the one transaction, as per the Majority Opinion, is $150. The net income in the two transactions, as per the Concurring Opinion, is also $150—$300 discharge of debt income minus $150 loss on the Real Estate transaction. However, in splitting the transaction in two, you can determine whether the gain is capital or ordinary (See Chapter X), and, if there was a loss, whether the loss was deductible (See Chapter V). Again, if the debt is *nonrecourse* and the debt exceeds the collateral, then *Tufts* applies, and there is one transaction. In contrast, if the debt is *recourse*, and the debt exceeds the collateral, then, according to the IRS, you use the two-transaction approach of the concurring opinion.

When the value of the collateral is greater than the amount of the debt, two things are true. First, it does not matter if the debt was *recourse* or *nonrecourse*. Second, there is no cancellation of indebtedness income, because the debt is fully paid. It may well be that part of the amount realized is the debt discharged, but the debt is still paid.

Consider that you have a basis of $25 in Blackacre. Its current fair market value is $400, subject to a debt of $100. You sell it to Buyer, who pays you $300, and assumes the debt. Your Amount Realized will be $400—the sum of the $300 cash and the $100 assumed debt—now discharged to you. Your basis is $25, and your gain is $375. The result is the same whether the debt was *recourse* or *nonrecourse*. In this instance, *Tufts* doesn't matter.

What Is Not Income?

So far, we have been talking about what **is** income. It's much more fun to talk about what **isn't** income. That leads us to a loving look at the five most wonderful words in the Code: **"Gross income does not include. . ."** Don't they just roll off the tongue in a delightful way?

A. Gifts and Bequests

§ 102.   Gifts and inheritances

(a)   General rule.—Gross income does not include the value of property acquired by gift, bequest, devise, or inheritance.

First of all, we are talking about "property acquired." The *recipient* of a gift, bequest, devise or inheritance will receive it free of the federal income tax, pursuant to the general rule of § 102(a). The one *making* the gift, or, for that matter, the dead guy who made the bequest, isn't covered. Those folks might have to pay tax pursuant to the Federal Gift Tax, the Federal Estate Tax, or state wealth transfer taxes. But this is the federal income tax we're talking about. The making of a gift or bequest is not an income taxable event to the donor or decedent. And the recipient gets it free of the income tax.

Why is the receipt of a gift, bequest, devise or inheritance tax free? Well, maybe it shouldn't be. But here are two reasons why perhaps it should.

First, even if the recipient isn't taxed, the donor or decedent might well be taxed under a different taxing regime. This reason is, frankly, not terribly persuasive. At least on the federal level, the Federal Estate and Gift Taxes have such a high taxfree threshold that hardly anyone pays them, except the superrich. And even the superrich can probably avoid a lot of them with decent lawyers.

Second, most of us live in family groups, but the Internal Revenue Code generally recognizes only individual taxpayers. So there's a disconnect between how we live—in families—and how we pay taxes—as individuals. This disconnect is perhaps most apparent in the case of transfers within the family unit. Who is most likely to give a gift or bequest to whom? Parents give gifts and bequests to their children. Therefore, gifts and bequests are, by and large, exactly such intrafamily transfers. Perhaps it is best if we exclude them from taxation. That's what § 102 generally does.

1.   *What Is a Gift or Bequest?*

The statute doesn't exactly tell us, does it? Luckily, the Supreme Court did, sort of. The leading case is Commissioner v. Duberstein, 363 U.S. 278 (1960). Here's what we know from the case:

- It's a question of fact
- It depends upon the motivation of the donor, not the donee
- It usually doesn't involve a quid pro quo; and

- It flows from detached and disinterested generosity.

A devise, inheritance, or bequest is defined the same way as a gift. It depends upon the transferor's intent. Only this time, the transferor is dead.

Applying these rules, one would think that a transfer of value from an Employer to an Employee would rarely be a gift. Most such transfers are salary. Most salary payments are not made out of detached and disinterested generosity. In fact, most of them are quid pro quo payments—salary for labor. Salary payments, therefore, are taxable income—not gifts.

However, one might imagine exceptions. Imagine that a well-loved, long-time Employee has become seriously ill, and can't afford the medical expenses. A payment from Employer to Employee in those circumstances does look like a gift. In fact, under prior law, there were many cases in which the taxpayers argued just that. However, Congress finally got tired of the arguments, and enacted § 102(c), which provides that

> Subsection (a) shall not exclude from gross income any amount transferred by or for an employer to, or for the benefit of, an employee.

That seems to end the matter, doesn't it? Of course not. What if Father employs Son, and Father gives Son a Christmas present or a birthday present. Is that present taxable? Probably not. Proposed Regulation § 1.102–1(f)(2) provides:

> For purposes of section 102(c), extraordinary transfers to the natural objects of an employer's bounty will not be considered transfers to, or for the benefit of, an employee if the employee can show that the transfer was not made in recognition of the employee's employment. Accordingly, section 102(c) shall not apply to amounts transferred between related parties (e.g., father and son)

if the purpose of the transfer can be substantially attributed to the familial relationship of the parties and not to the circumstances of their employment.

Feel better now?

2.   *Basis in Gifted Property*

Generally speaking, your basis in property is the amount you paid for it. But, when you receive a gift, you didn't pay for it. So, should your basis be zero?

No. According to Section 1015, your basis in gifted property depends on

- whether it went up in value since donor acquired it, or down

- what the donee is selling it for, and

- whether gift tax was paid when the gift was made.

In order to keep this book short and happy, we're going to ignore the gift tax part.

Let's say donor bought the property for $500, and, when it was worth $750, donor gifted it to donee. In that case, when donee sells it, donee's basis will be the same as donor's old basis, which is $500. Period. If the fair market value of the gifted asset at the time of the gift (here $750) is greater than donor's basis (here $500), then donor's basis of $500 carries over to donee.

Let's say donor bought the property for $500, and, when it was worth $300, donor gifted it to donee. In that case, we need to know whether donee is selling the property for a gain, or for a loss. Let's say that donee sells the property for $1,250. That means that donee is selling the property for a gain, no matter how you slice it. In that event, donor's basis of $500 again carries over to donee. Whenever donee sells the property for a gain, donor's basis carries over.

Amount realized	$1,250
- Basis	$500
Gain	$750

Let's say, on the other hand, that donee sells the property for $100. That's a loss, no matter how you slice it. In that event, donee's basis will be the fair market value of the property at the time of the gift, or $300. The loss will be:

Amount realized	$100
- Basis	$300
Gain/loss	($200)

Is that $200 loss deductible? It depends. If it's a business loss, it's deductible. If it's a personal loss, probably not. We'll talk more about this when we get to deductions.

Let's say the donor sells the property for $450. Now, we don't know if it's a gain or a loss. If you use donor's old basis of $500, it looks like a loss [$450 Amount Realized is less than $500 basis]. However, if you use the fair market value at the time of the gift ($300), it looks like a gain [$450 Amount Realized is greater than $300 basis]. So what do you do?

There is no gain, and no loss. The sale is not a taxable event, and the new buyer picks up a basis of $450—what she paid for the property. This happens whenever the donee sells for a price between donor's old basis and the fair market value of the property at the time of the gift.

3. Basis in Bequeathed Property

According to § 1014, the basis of property acquired from a decedent is the fair market value of the property on the date of decedent's death. Alternatively, it is the value of the property for estate tax purposes. Usually, that's pretty much the same value.

Say decedent purchased the property in 1990 for $400,000. When decedent passed away in 2010, the property was worth $500,000. Decedent's Beneficiary sells the property in 2015 for $550,000. Beneficiary will recognize taxable gain of $50,000:

Amount realized	$550,000
- Basis	$500,000
Gain	$50,000

Since Decedent acquired it, the property has appreciated by $150,000—from $400,000 to $550,000. However, Beneficiary only recognizes gain of $50,000. Nobody, alive or dead, recognizes the other $100,000 of gain. That's because the basis is "stepped up" from Decedent's basis to the fair market value of the property at the time of Decedent's death.

This makes no sense. In fact, Congress tried to change it in 1976, but failed. Once you put a tax break into the Code, it's pretty hard to get rid of it. The § 1014 step up in basis is an additional, hugely important advantage that property owners enjoy. If their property goes up in value, and if they are lucky enough to die while they still hold it, then no one pays the tax on the appreciation that occurred during their lifetimes.

Here's a neat scheme. Son purchases Whiteacre for $400,000 in 1990. In 2010, when it is worth $500,000, he gifts it to Father. Father is not exactly in the best of health at the time. Father dies six months later, willing all of his worldly goods, including Whiteacre, back to Son. Son would like to take a stepped up basis of $500,000 in Whiteacre. Can he do so?

No. Congress doesn't always figure everything out, but they caught this one. Section 1014(e) says that, in that situation, because the donee Father died within a year after the gift of the appreciated property was made, Son's basis is not stepped up. Rather, Son's basis will be $400,000.

Nice try. The trick is to make sure that the old geezer lasts for a year or more after the gift.

4. *Tips*

You might think that tips should be taxfree gifts, flowing from detached and disinterested generosity. They are not. Tips are taxable compensation.

Those who receive tips, and those who employ them, have not always been cooperative about reporting the income. As a result, Congress enacted § 6053. Pursuant to the statute, the tip rate in "large food or beverage establishments" is presumed to be 8%. If the aggregate tips reported in such establishments are less than 8%, then the tipped employees will be taxed on the 8% anyway, with the deficiency to be allocated among to employees as the employer (the restaurant owner) sees fit.

Our elected representatives are servants of the people. As such, they are always anxious to hear from their constituents. Here is one letter received from a waitress after the enactment of § 6053:

Death to the IRS! Take your eight percent on tips and stick it up your ass.

B. Life Insurance

§ 101. Certain death benefits

(a) Proceeds of life insurance contracts payable by reason of death—

(1) General rule.—Except as otherwise provided in paragraph two, subsection (d), subsection (f)

and subsection (j), gross income does not include amounts received (whether in a single sum or otherwise) under a life insurance contract, if such amounts are paid by reason of the death of the insured.

Let's tick off a few things we know from the statute:

- There's a general rule, and there are exceptions

- To exclude an amount under the general rule, the amount must be received under a life insurance contract; and

- To exclude an amount under the general rule, the amount must be paid by reason of the death of the insured.

Who buys life insurance for whom? Generally, family members buy it for other family members. What is life insurance, then? Life insurance is essentially a bequest, except that it is funded through a life insurance investment. If the receipt of bequests is taxfree, then the receipt of life insurance should be taxfree as well, and it is.

However, that holds true only when the life insurance is actually used as a bequest. What if I take out a life insurance policy, and then sell it for a profit? Now, I'm not using the life insurance policy to fund a bequest. Instead, I'm using it just like any other investment. Accordingly, I will be taxed on my profit. Note that those sales proceeds will not be an "amount paid by reason of the death of the insured." Therefore, the general rule of § 101 does not apply.

There's just one other thing about life insurance, however. Say Jack and June, each aged 25, have $100,000 in cash. Jack puts his in the bank, earning interest. June uses hers to buy a life insurance policy, with a face amount of $500,000. She pays a single premium of, you guessed it, $100,000.

Both Jack and June live for another 50 years. When Jack dies at age 75, his savings account has grown to $500,000, which he wills to his daughter, Jacqueline. When June dies at age 75, the $500,000 in life insurance proceeds goes to her daughter, Juno.

	Jack	June
Age 25	$100,000 cash	$100,000 cash
50 Years	Bank savings accounts grows to $500,000	Buy $500,000 life insurance policy for a single premium of $100,000
Death at 75	$500,000 by will to Daughter, Jacqueline	$500,000 insurance proceeds to Daughter, Juno

The tax consequences at death are pretty comparable. Jack's daughter, Jacqueline, gets $500,000 taxfree as a bequest under § 102. June's daughter, Juno, gets the $500,000 life insurance proceeds taxfree under § 101. But what about that 50-year period? During that 50 years, Jack's bank savings account grew because the bank paid interest. Taxable interest. Arguably, June's life insurance policy grew as well. June paid $100,000 for it, and it kicked out $500,000 of proceeds to Juno. But nobody pays any tax on that "internal growth." Why not?

C. Fringe Benefits

To the tax lawyer, fringe benefits are as good as it gets. They are, generally speaking, deductible to the employer, but they are taxfree to the employee. What could be better than that?

1. Section 132

The first taxfree fringe benefits came with the railroads. Passenger railroads, even in their heyday, rarely filled every seat. So, with available empty seats, it made perfect sense to allow the railroad employees to ride for free. It really didn't cost the railroads anything. And the government went along. It seemed to be such a sensible idea; why spoil it by taxing it?

That was the beginning. Over time, more and more taxfree fringe benefits were added. Once they were in, it was awfully hard to get them out. Congress tried many times, and failed. Finally, they enacted § 132—not to eliminate any fringe benefits, but merely to codify them, in the hope that the legislation would freeze things, and not allow any more tax free fringe benefits to develop.

§ 132.   Certain fringe benefits

(a)   Exclusion from gross income.—Gross income shall not include any fringe benefit which qualifies as a—

. . .

Subsection 132(a) is the operative subsection, providing that, if an item fits into one of the listed categories, then it is excluded. Subsections (b) through (g) give further definitions of the listed categories. The rest of the statute contains further definitions, and special rules. Let's have a look at some of the major categories.

a.   No Additional Cost Service §§ 132(a)(1) and 132(b)

This one harks back to those railroad employees. But let's get a bit more modern. Imagine an airline employee who gets to fly for free, provided that there is an empty, unsold seat. The value of that flight is taxfree as a no additional cost service. It really doesn't cost the airline anything to allow the employee to use that seat, so why shouldn't they provide this benefit?

b.   Qualified Employee Discounts §§ 132(a)(2) and 132(c)

For goods, a qualified employee discount is taxfree as long as the employee pays at least wholesale. For services, the discount is taxfree as long as it doesn't exceed 20%.

This would be a good time to look at § 132(j)(1)—the nondiscrimination rule. Note that it applies only to paragraphs (1) and (2) of subsection (a). That means that it applies only to no additional cost services and qualified employee discounts. Those two fringe benefits are taxfree only if they do not discriminate in favor of the highly paid employees.

c.   Working Condition Fringes §§ 132(a)(3) and 132(d)

Imagine that you apply for a job at the local steel mill. You discuss wages and hours, and everything looks great. The Hiring Guy tells you that the job is yours if you want it, but there's just one thing—you're going to have to provide your own steel mill. So, you go out and rent yourself a steel mill. If you were dumb enough to do that, the steel mill rental would be deductible to you. [However, if you were indeed an employee, the steel mill rental expense would be a nondeductible employee business expense, from now until 2025. See Chapter VIII.]

Since rental of the steel mill, had you paid it yourself, should theoretically have been deductible by you as a business expense, the steel mill, when provided to you by your employer, will be tax free. That's a working condition fringe benefit. For example, the value of an associate's office, provided to her for free by the law firm, is a taxfree working condition fringe benefit to the lucky associate.

2. *Section 119*

§ 119.   Meals or lodging furnished for the convenience of the employer

(a)   Meals and lodging furnished to an employee, his spouse, and his dependents, pursuant to employment—There shall be excluded from gross income of an employee the value of any meals or lodging furnished to him, his spouse, or any of his dependents by or on behalf of his employer for the convenience of the employer but only if—

   (1)   In the case of meals, the meals are furnished on the business premises of the employer, or

   (2)   In the case of lodging, the employee is required to accept such lodging on the business premises of his employer as a condition of his employment.

Note that the "convenience of the employer" requirement can be found in the general language of § 132(a), before it gets to the specific requirements of (a)(1) for meals, and (a)(2) for lodging. Therefore, the "convenience of the employer" requirement applies to both meals and lodging. What does "convenience of the employer" mean? It's hard to say precisely—it's a caselaw kind of thing. But you might consider that, if you can show that the employer was better off by providing these meals and lodging in kind, rather than providing that much more salary in cash, that probably means that providing the meals and lodging were for the convenience of the employer. Think of a fire department providing free meals and lodging to the fireman at the firehouse. If the firemen ae already at the firehouse, then they can respond to the fire alarm much more quickly.

So, for free meals, there are two requirements:

- Convenience of the employer

- Business premises.

For lodging, there appear to be three requirements:

- Convenience of the employer

- Business premises

- Required to accept as a condition of employment.

But what about that third one? Doesn't that suggest a bit of collusion? Employee wants taxfree housing, so she asks employer to require her to accept them as a condition of employment. Employer couldn't care less, so he says okay. Caselaw suggests that that third requirement is illusory, and is really covered by the convenience of the employer requirement.

D. Scholarships and Fellowships

§ 117.   Qualified scholarships

(a)   General rule.—Gross income does not include any amount received as a qualified scholarship by an individual who is a candidate for a degree at an educational organization described in section 170(b)(1)(a)(II).

You're probably dying to know what a "qualified scholarship" is. It's defined in § 117(b). Basically, it's a scholarship for tuition and related expenses. Note, however, that you lose the taxfree status if the amounts are paid for services required as a condition for receiving the qualified scholarship. See § 117(c)(1). Such payments look too much like compensation for services.

Then there are qualified tuition reductions, pursuant to § 117(d). If an educational organization provides for a tuition reduction for its employees, or certain family members of the employees, they are also taxfree. Such qualified tuition reductions must be for education below the graduate level (unless the employee is a teaching or research assistant as described in § 117(d)(5)), and they may not discriminate in favor of highly compensated employees.

What about athletic scholarships? Some have argued that college athletes, especially in the major sports, are actually paid employees of their institutions. The education provided to them, it is argued, is a joke. Their "scholarships," they say, should be taxable compensation income.

Arguably, the motivations of the granting institutions are similar, whether the scholarships be athletic or academic. In the case of athletic scholarships, colleges are acting out of pecuniary motivation. They "buy" the best athletes, because success on the playing fields will generate direct revenue from tickets, television contracts, etc. In addition, it will increase name recognition of the school, thus increasing applications for admission across the board, making the school more popular for faculty, etc. If the athlete in question does not measure up to his or her athletic potential, the scholarship might not be renewed for another year.

Academic scholarships are similar. "Buying" good academic students increases the academic reputation of the school, increasing applications, making the school more popular with faculty. The success of the "bought" student in later life has two pecuniary benefits. First, the student herself might feel grateful enough to give back to the school. Second, other students will want to go and duplicate that success. Of course, if the "bought" student does not pan out, in terms of a stated grade point average, the scholarship is not renewed.

Given their similarity, either all scholarships—whether academic or athletic—should be taxable, or all scholarships should be taxfree. According to § 117, they are all taxfree. Perhaps we are finessing the tax issues in light of the societal benefits that all scholarships provide.

E. Damages

What if you sue someone and win? If you won, that other person must have done you wrong, somehow. The damages you collect, whether by court judgment or by settlement, can be seen as putting you back to where you were before the defendant did you wrong. What if, for example, defendant agreed to hire you, and then reneged. If you sue, and win, the damages will be a replacement for the wages the defendant should have paid you. Those wages would have been taxable, so the damages paid in lieu of those wages will be taxable as well.

What if defendant negligently broke a vase in your pottery shop? The damages you will receive will be a replacement for the profit you should have made when you sold the vase ["You broke it— you bought it."]. That profit would have been taxable, so the damages will be taxable as well.

Damages can be seen as a replacement for something else— intended to put you back where you should have been, before the defendant did you wrong. If the item replaced by the damage award would have been taxable, then the damages should be taxable. If that item would have been taxfree, then the damages should be taxfree as well.

Why are we discussing damages in Chapter IV? Because many damage awards are taxfree. Consider. You're walking down the street, enjoying the use of your two legs. Defendant negligently hits you with her car. As a result, your legs are amputated. You sue. The damages are intended to compensate you for the loss of the ability to use your legs. They are supposed to put you back in the place you were in before. Of course, they can't do that completely, but we do what we can.

Where were you before the accident? You had the use of your legs. Having the use of your legs is not a taxable event. If the use of your legs is not taxable, then a payment intended to replace having the use of your legs shouldn't be taxable either. And it isn't. Damages on account of personal, physical injuries—perhaps the most common type of damages—are tax free.

Now, here's where things get tricky. There's a statute. Don't statutes just ruin everything? This time, it's Section 104(a)(2)

§ 104.   Compensation for injuries or sickness

(a) In general.—Except . . . gross income does not include—

* * *

(2) The amount of any damages (other than punitive damages) received (whether by suit or agreement and whether as lump sums or as periodic payments) on account of personal physical injuries or physical sickness.

(3)

(4)

(5)

. . .

> For purposes of paragraph (2), emotional
> distress shall not be treated as a physical injury
> or physical sickness.

Say you were injured in an automobile accident. You sue for pain and suffering, and lost wages. The pain and suffering would have been taxfree without the statute, because they are intended to replace the condition of not being in pain, which is not a taxable condition.

But what about the lost wages? Without the accident, you would have continued to work, and those wages would have been taxable. Therefore the lost wages damage award, as a substitute for what would have been taxable wages, should also be taxable. But they are not. Section 104(a)(2) exempts **any** damages on account of personal physical injuries, so that includes the lost wages.

The taxation of damages should be important to you as lawyers, even if you have no desire to practice tax law. If you represent plaintiffs, you had better be able to tell them whether any damage or settlement awards received will be taxable. If you can't, it would be best if you at least realize that the issue exists, so that you can consult someone else.

Notice also that it is possible to sue for multiple elements of damages, some of which might be taxable, and others of which might be taxfree. If you win, make sure that the court damage award, or the settlement agreement, provides an allocation of the damages into those two categories, so that you don't have to fight IRS over the tax issues.

CHAPTER V

Business Deductions

A. General Introduction

Let's review the basic arithmetic of the tax laws. Items of income are **added** to the taxable amount. Deductions are **subtracted** from the taxable amount. Trust me—subtraction is better.

The clearest case for subtraction is when you have business expenses. Take Sam, who is the beneficiary of a trust, and Dave, a lawyer. Sam receives $200,000 of trust income this year. Dave earns $200,000 in legal fees. However, Dave has to pay $50,000 in salary to his secretary, and $35,000 rent on his office. That's $85,000 in expenses incurred to generate that $200,000 in legal fees.

Sam's disposable income [what he can actually spend however he wants] is:

Trust income	$200,000
Expenses	- $0
Disposable Income	$200,000

Dave's disposable income is:

Legal fees	$200,000
Expenses	- $85,000
Disposable income	$115,000

Surely, it wouldn't be fair to tax both Sam and Dave on the $200,000, when Sam can really use all of it, and Dave can't. Our tax laws don't do that. They recognize that it takes money to make money, and they allow business expenses to be deductible. Sam will be taxed on $200,000, but Dave will be taxed on only $115,000.

What about nonbusiness expenses? What about food, for example. If I stopped eating, I'd eventually have to stop working. Therefore, it is absolutely necessary for me to incur my food expenses, if I am to keep earning money. So, should my food be deductible? No.

Here's the thing. I'd have to keep eating even if I weren't working. Everyone—working or not—spends money on food. Allowing a deduction for food expenses would be allowing the same deduction for everyone. It wouldn't distinguish one taxpayer from another, which, after all, is why we use the income measurement in the first place.

But wait, there's more. Not everyone spends the same on food. Some people eat PB&J, and some eat caviar. If all food were deductible, then the ones who ate caviar would deduct more than the ones who ate PB&J. In fact, the tax laws would encourage people to eat caviar. That would be silly. Lifestyle choices shouldn't affect your tax bill. Taxes should be levied on your ability to pay, measured by your income. They should not be measured by what you do with your income.

So, as a general rule, business expenses are deductible, and nonbusiness expenses are nondeductible. Of course, that means that the line between business and nonbusiness becomes very important. What about those expenses which are mixed motive— part business and part personal? Those deserve special consideration. See Chapter VIII. Then again, what about personal expenses? They should be nondeductible, unless there's an awfully good reason to deduct them. Sometimes there is. See Chapter VII.

B. Section 162

§ 162.   Trade or business expenses

There shall be allowed as a deduction all the ordinary and necessary expenses paid or incurred during the taxable year in carrying on any trade or business. . .

What do we know so far? First, the expenses must be "ordinary and necessary." Now, you might think that "necessary" means absolutely crucial, as in "It is necessary for me to breathe in order to live." Well, it doesn't mean that. "Necessary" means "appropriate and helpful," according to Welch v. Helvering, 290 U.S. 111 (1933). As it turns out, "necessary" is not much of a problem. "Ordinary" is a problem, but we'll get to that later.

"Paid or incurred" means that you can deduct these expenses if you are on the cash basis of accounting ("paid"), or the accrual basis ("incurred"). See Chapter IX. Don't worry about that now.

"Carrying on" relates back to "during the taxable year." You must already be "carrying on" the trade or business during the taxable year in question. Let's say, for example, that you want to publish a newspaper, so you travel around the country looking for a newspaper business to buy. You are incurring travel expenses all right, but you are not yet carrying on a trade or business. You might get your deductions from other section of the Code, but not § 162.

Of course, the big gorilla in the room is "trade or business." We don't really know exactly what a "trade or business" is. We do know that you have to take your activity seriously, and that you have to spend some pretty regular hours at it. We also know that, generally speaking, managing your own stock and bond investments is not carrying on a trade or business, no matter how seriously you take it, and no matter how much time you spend on it. See Higgins v. Commissioner, 312 U.S. 212 (1941). Congress was so irked by *Higgins* that they enacted a new section of the Code—212—which says that managing your own investment property may well not be a trade or business under Section 162, but it will be deductible anyway, under new section 212.

Okay, back to "ordinary." "Ordinary" has many meanings. An ordinary expense is not a capital expense. See Chapter VI for that one. It is common, in the sense that other businesses in the same time and place and circumstance incur similar expenses. It also can't be too personal, for then it would not be an "ordinary business" expense. All of this is a mite vague, but don't worry. Like so much in law, most cases are easy, and it only gets fuzzy at the margins. Reasonable salaries, business travel, and rent are easy cases, specifically listed in § 162(a)(1) through (3).

1. *Must Business Deductions Be Reasonable?*

The word "reasonable" occurs in subsection 162(a)(1), dealing with salaries, rather than in the general language of § 162(a). Similarly, "lavish or extravagant" appears in subsection 162(a)(2), dealing with travel expenses, rather than in the general language of § 162(a). You can deduce that, to be deductible, salaries must be reasonable, but other business expenses need not. Travel expenses must not be lavish or extravagant, but other business expenses can be. Let's talk about the special cases of salaries and travel expenses later. [Salaries are addressed in this chapter, below. Travel Expenses are addressed in Chapter VIII.] For now, focus on the fact that other business expenses can be unreasonable, or even lavish or extravagant, and still be deductible. Aren't we encouraging foolish behavior by this provision of the tax code?

Well, maybe. But consider. These are business expenses. The whole point of incurring a business expense is to make a profit. If you spend more on your business expenses—if your business expenses are unreasonable, or even lavish or extravagant—you make less profit. In the worst case scenario, you might even go bankrupt. You don't need the tax code to regulate these types of dumb behavior. The market will do it for us.

2. Salaries

a. In General

To understand the treatment of salaries, you need to compare them to dividends. Salaries are deductible to the employer. Dividends, however, are not deductible to the corporate payor. When a corporation pays dividends to its shareholders, it is merely sharing its profits with its owners. It is not incurring a deductible expense.

Imagine that one of the corporation's shareholders is also an employee of the corporation. The corporation would like to pay that individual, but how it does so makes a huge difference. If the payment is a dividend, then it is not deductible to the corporation, but it is still taxable to the individual. That's two taxes.

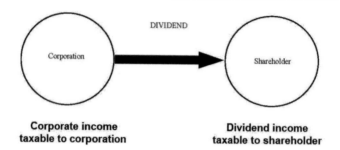

Corporate income
taxable to corporation
         Dividend income
         taxable to shareholder

If, however, the payment is salary, then it is deductible to the corporation. That wipes out the taxable income at the corporate level. The salary is still taxable to the employee, but that's one tax, not two.

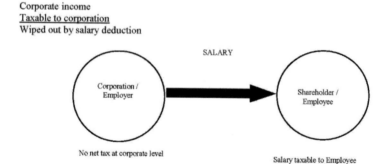

Therefore, it is very much in the interests of the corporation to characterize a payment to that individual as salary, rather than as a dividend. That being said, it is highly likely that, if the salary payment is unreasonably high, then part of the payment is really a dividend in disguise.

Imagine that the corporation has two employees—A and B. A and B do exactly the same job, and they do it equally well. However, A is also a shareholder, but B is not. The corporation pays A a salary of $50,000, and B a salary of $40,000. Why is the corporation paying A $10,000 more salary than B? It seems likely that the payment to A is really $40,000 in salary and $10,000 in dividends. The corporation is trying to disguise that extra $10,000 payment as salary, so that it can deduct it. Therefore, § 162(a)(1) limits the deduction for salary to what is reasonable, for fear that unreasonably high salary payments might be disguised dividends.

What if the employee in question is not a shareholder? In that event, there is no worry that the payment might be a dividend in disguise. However, the reasonableness limitation applies to all employees, whether or not they are shareholders. Could one argue that the statute only applies to shareholders, to bring about the apparent legislative intent? No. Since the statute is clear on its face, legislative intent is irrelevant.

How do you determine the reasonableness of the compensation? Caselaw would suggest that you use a multiple factor test. Presumably, the most relevant inquiry would be what comparable employees are being paid by other employers.

Incentive compensation schemes are different. Say an employee agrees to be paid 10% of company profits each year. That, of course, is a bit of a gamble for both parties. If the company earns nothing, then the employee does not get paid. On the other hand, if the company has a terrific year, then the employee gets paid an exorbitant salary—perhaps much more than was deserved.

To determine the reasonableness of an incentive compensation salary for the purposes of § 162(a)(1), go through a two-step process. First, is the salary reasonable in absolute terms? If so, then it is deductible. If not, then go to the second step. Even if the salary was unreasonably high, was the incentive compensation scheme that created it the result of a free bargain between employer and employee? If so, then the resulting salary is reasonable, nonetheless.

b. The Million Dollar Cap

To be deductible, salary must not only be reasonable—it must also not exceed one million dollars. See § 162(m). Does this further restriction make any sense? Shouldn't the marketplace generally control the amounts of salaries? If an executive is overpaid, one would think that the company profits would go down, and the shareholders would force the Board of Directors either to fire the executive or to lower the salary. However, some might argue that power is so diffuse in corporations, and the corporate boards are so intertwined, that one cannot rely upon these forces of the marketplace and shareholder democracy to work.

In any event, it is easy to get around the million dollar cap with incentive compensation schemes. See § 162(m)(4)(B) and (C). Furthermore, wouldn't it make more sense to have a restriction on executives making too high a multiple of the compensation of the lowest employee, rather than a flat figure?

3. *The Public Policy Doctrine and Weed*

In Commissioner v. Sullivan, 356 U.S. 27 (1958), the taxpayer was an illegal bookie. He got busted, and taxed. He argued that, if he was to be taxed on his illegal income, at least he should have been allowed to deduct the expenses of earning that income. The Supreme Court agreed. If you do the crime, you should do the time. However, it shouldn't mean that your taxes are computed any differently. Legal income is taxable; illegal income is taxable. It should follow that the expenses of either are deductible.

On the same day, the Supreme Court decided Tank Truck Rentals, Inc. v. Commissioner, 356 U.S. 30 (1958). In *Tank Truck*, the taxpayer knowingly violated the weight limit laws with its trucks. When it was caught, it paid the fine. Now it wanted to deduct the fines as an ordinary and necessary business expense. The Supreme Court said no. The fines were enacted as a legitimate part of the police power of the state. If those fines were deductible, then the federal government would be alleviating the penalty that the state government had enacted, thus impinging on the **public**

policy of the state. That would violate the comity between the federal and state governments. Business expenses, then, are deductible, whether the underlying business is legal or illegal, unless the **public policy doctrine** comes into play.

The guts of the public policy doctrine is found in § 162(f) which says that fines are nondeductible. However, there is a possible, broader caselaw notion, which suggests that, when there is a clearly delineated policy of a state, that policy cannot be alleviated by federal tax law.

Now let's talk weed. In 1970, Jeffrey Edmondson, a drug dealer, was busted. The IRS taxed him on his drug-related income. Edmondson pointed out that, if he was to pay tax on his drug-related income, he should be allowed to deduct his drug-related expenses. His drug business, as it happened, covered a multi-state area, so he had travelling expenses. Furthermore, as a self-respecting drug dealer, he had purchased a really accurate scale. The cost of the scale was a legitimate business expense, he argued. The Tax Court agreed, and allowed his deductions.

Congress was horrified, and enacted Section 280E, which provides:

> No deduction or credit shall be allowed for any amount paid or incurred during the taxable year in carrying on any trade or business if such trade or business (or the activities which comprise such trade or business) consists of trafficking in controlled substances (within the meaning of schedule I and II of the Controlled Substances Act) which is prohibited by Federal law or the law of any State in which such trade or business is conducted.

Section 280E was dumb enough when it was passed. Now, however, with medical marijuana legal in lots of states, and recreational marijuana legal in a few, things are getting really interesting. What if you are a medical marijuana dispensary in, say, California? Your business is legal in California, but still illegal under federal law. Of course you have to pay federal taxes on your income, but can you deduct your expenses? Section 280E says no.

Recent caselaw recognizes that a medical marijuana dispensary might be engaged in more than one business. If so, then the expenses allocable to the marijuana might be nondeductible, but the expenses allocable to the other businesses—say group therapy sessions—might be deductible. Olive v. Commissioner, 792 F.3d 1146 (9th Cir. 2015), suggests that such a dispensary would be engaged in the multiple businesses only if the dispensary charged separately for the two kinds of goods and services. So, the message is clear. Dispense medical marijuana, and charge for it. Also, provide other goods and services, and charge for them. Now you're engaged in multiple businesses. If you can get a favorable allocation ratio, then you can deduct a lot of your expenses. Stay tuned.

4. Causation

We will talk later about mixed motive expenses—personal and business. See Chapter VIII. Those are usually bifurcated, somehow. But what about an expense that seems to have a personal cause and a business cause? Well, which is it?

The Supreme Court addressed this issue, sort of, in Gilmore v. United States, 372 U.S. 39 (1963). Mr. Gilmore and his wife got a divorce. By the way, the allegations in the divorce case were pretty spectacular. See Joel Newman, *Gilmore v. United States: The Divorce* 116 Tax Notes 493 (August 6, 2007).

Of course, marriage is personal, and so is divorce. Expenses incurred to get a divorce, or to litigate one, are also personal. But Mr. Gilmore had a different argument. He owned three car dealerships. He argued that, if his wife, Dixie, had won in divorce court, then she would have been awarded all of his stock in his corporations, whereupon, she would fire him. Further, if her sensational allegations had been accepted by the Court, General Motors could have applied a morals clause, and canceled his franchises. Therefore, Mr. Gilmore argued that he incurred the divorce expenses in order to save his job. These were business expenses, he said, so his divorce litigation costs were deductible.

The Supreme Court said no. They said that it is the **origin of the expense** that counts, not the **consequence**. In Mr. Gilmore's case, the **origin** of the expense was his marital troubles with Dixie. They were personal. The prospect of the loss of his employment or his franchise was, in contrast, a **consequence** of the expenses—rather than their origin.

The Court imagined two drivers, both of whom had accidents during personal trips, and were sued. One had a business that was put at risk by the lawsuit; the other did not. The possible business consequence should not matter, said the Court. The important inquiry is to the origin of the expense. Expenses that have a personal origin should be nondeductible, no matter what the consequences of the expense might be. Both drivers incurred nondeductible, personal expenses.

This doctrine has turned out to be well-nigh incoherent. This is especially true if you consider that the happenstance of naming a corporate defendant in a lawsuit can make an expense a business expense, and therefore deductible, even though the origin of the expense was otherwise completely personal.

CHAPTER VI

Capital Recovery

When you buy Blackacre for $100,000, you have invested capital of $100,000. When you later sell for $125,000, you subtract your basis of $100,000 from your amount realized of $125,000. In doing so, you are recovering your $100,000 capital investment, taxfree. This chapter is about that recovery of capital. Mostly, it is about when you can do so.

A. The Matching Principle

Let's say you own a business that earns a million dollars a year. This year, you buy some ink for your printer for $25, and you buy a new building for $1,000,000. Both of these payments are undeniably geared to help you make money. Both of them should be above-the-line business deductions. But when do you take them into account?

The $25 worth of ink is easy. The ink will last, say, one month. So, you spend the $25 this year. You use it up this year. Any impact that the expenditure has on your bottom line will be this year. So, you should deduct it this year.

The building is different. Let's say that the building will last 25 years. When should you take that million dollar expenditure into account? Well, you spent the money in Year 1. You could deduct all of it then. Alternatively, you spent that million dollars to acquire an asset—the building. Let's say that, after 25 years, the building is pretty worthless, so you sell it for a penny.

Amount realized:	$.01
– Basis	$1,000,000.00
Loss	($999,999.99)

So, you take the loss in Year 25.

Finally, you could spread the cost of the building over its 25-year useful life. The cost of the building – $1,000,000—divided by its useful life gives you $40,000 per year.

The question is as much one of accounting as of tax. Remember, one of the functions of accounting is to look at how your business is doing. Let's consider the three alternatives:

1. Deduct the $1,000,000 in Year 1

	Year 1	Year 2-24	Year 25
Income	$1,000,000	$1,000,000	$1,000,000
Expense	$1,000,000	$0	$0
Profit/loss	$0	$1,000,000	$1,000,000

Looks like Year 1 was a disaster, but Years 2-24 were really good.

2. Deduct the Loss in Year 25

	Year 1	Year 2-24	Year 25
Income	$1,000,000	$1,000,000	$1,000,000
Expense	$0	$0	-999,999.99
Profit/loss	$1,000,000	$1,000,000	$.01

Looks like Years 1-24 were really good, but Year 25 was a disaster.

3. Spread out the Expense over the Building's Useful Life

	Year 1	Year 2-24	Year 25
Income	$1,000,000	$1,000,000	$1,000,000
Expense	$40,000	$40,000	$40,000
Profit/Loss	$960,000	$960,000	$960,000

Looks like all 25 years were okay.

Clearly, the third method gives you the best picture of what happened. And that's what we use, both for accounting purposes, and for tax. The principle is to match the expenses with the income generated by those expenses. If, as here, the expenses were likely to generate income for 25 years, then the deductions for those expenses should be spread out over 25 years as well.

So, when do you deduct your entire expense in the year it is incurred? The **matching principle** would tell us that you deduct it all when that expense is expected to generate income for less than a year. When, in contrast, the expense is expected to generate income for more than a year, you don't deduct it all in the year incurred. Instead, you **capitalize** the expense, and spread the deductions out over time.

That's what the matching principle would tell us. The reality of tax practice, however, is a bit different. For example, **maintenance and repairs** are deductible immediately. **Replacements** are capitalized. If you own a business building, and you replace one shingle on the roof, that's a repair, deductible immediately. However, if you replace the entire roof, that's capitalized.

Now I know you're thinking, "Wait a minute! First of all, that shingle was 'replaced.' Secondly, that replaced shingle will be good for 25 years. That's way more than one year. Why don't you have to capitalize it?"

As I said before, repairs are deducted immediately. Fixing, or replacing, one shingle is what all of us would call repair. So it's deductible immediately. Go figure.

So what, then, are replacements? Replacements are large expenditures, compared to the cost of the asset in question. They typically don't happen as often as repairs. Also, replacements increase the useful life, and the market value, of the asset in question. You might argue that maintenance and repairs also increase useful life and value, in that, if you don't do proper maintenance and repairs, you shorten the life of the asset, and its value declines. But here's the thing. Replacements increase the value and the useful life of an asset, over what they would normally have been, given proper maintenance and repair.

Distinguishing repairs and maintenance from replacements, or distinguishing immediately deductible expenses from capitalized expenses, can be tricky, as you can see. The IRS has recently promulgated voluminous new regulations on the subject. Good luck with that.

Immediate deduction you know. But how does capitalizing expenses actually work? Well, in the case of that million dollar building, you create a million dollar basis in your new asset—the building. Then, you actually spread out the deductions through depreciation.

B. Depreciation

1. In General

Stuff wears out. In fact, every physical thing in the universe will eventually wear out. We need to take that into account.

As things wear out, their market value usually declines. But not always. Some things, like rare old violins, continue to increase in value, even as they age. But they are still wearing out physically, so they are still depreciable. An asset does not have to decline in market value to be depreciable.

You cannot deduct depreciation, however, on your personal assets. Yes, they wear out, too, but the depreciation of personal assets is a personal expense. Personal expenses are not deductible. Therefore, for the remainder of this discussion, we are talking about property used in the trade or business (as described in § 162), or investment property (as described in § 212).

2. Mechanics

Here's the old, sort of easy way—straight line depreciation. Say you buy a machine for your business for $100. It will be useful to you in your business for 10 years. At the end of 10 years, you will be able to sell it for scrap metal for $20. Your allowable depreciation, then, is

Initial cost (otherwise known as basis)	$100
- Scrap value	$20
Allowable depreciation	$80

To take your $80 of allowable depreciation over ten years, you simply divide.

$$\frac{\text{Allowable depreciation} \quad \$80}{\text{Useful life} \qquad\qquad 10 \text{ years}} = \text{Annual depreciation of } \$8$$

However, Congress decided that straight line depreciation wasn't fast enough. Further, there were too many arguments about useful life and salvage value. So, Congress "simplified" it. You might have to use straight line, anyway, but for most things, there are faster, juicier methods. Forget about actual useful life. Forget about scrap value as well. Depending upon the nature of your property, you might be allowed to depreciate your entire basis over as little as 3 years. Heck, as if that weren't good enough, now some properties are eligible for immediate expensing. That means you can deduct the entire purchase price in the same year that you bought the property! For the details, go to an accountant. That's what they're there for.

3. *Depreciation and Basis*

Let's say that you used that business asset described above for four years. You deducted $8 of depreciation in each of those four years, for a total of $32 in depreciation deductions. Then you sold it for $68.

Amount realized	$68
- Basis	$100
Gain/loss	($32)

Wait a minute. That can't be right. You can't get $32 in depreciation deductions, and then take a $32 loss as well.

In fact, you don't. Your basis is adjusted downward for each dollar of depreciation allowed. Therefore your adjusted basis is:

Original basis	$100
- Depreciation adjustment	$32
Adjusted basis	$68

Now, when you sell for $68, there is no further loss:

Amount realized	$68
- Adjusted basis	$68
Gain/loss	$0

What if you sold the same asset at the same time for $90?

Amount realized	$90
- Adjusted basis	$68
Gain/loss	$22

Recall that you bought that asset for $100, and sold it for $90. You sold it for $10 less than what you paid for it. Now, net out the tax consequences. You took $32 in depreciation deductions, and, on sale, you recognized a $22 gain. Your deductions exceeded your gain by $10. That corresponds exactly to your $10 actual loss.

Well, perhaps not quite. As you will learn later, your $22 in gain might be taxed at favorable capital gains rates (or quasi-capital gains rates. See Chapter X), while your depreciation deductions are taken against ordinary income. They don't quite match up. However, through the magic of recapture, that $22 in gain will be recharacterized as ordinary gain, so everything works out.

C Annuities

Say you buy an annuity at age 25. You pay the annuity company $100,000, and they promise to pay you $3,000 a year for as long as you live. Your life expectancy is 50 years. Say you live just long enough to receive 50 payments. Fifty payments of $3,000 each equals $150,000. So you paid $100,000 and got $150,000 back. That's a profit of $50,000. When do you take that profit into income?

Section 72(a) says that annuity payments are taxable income. However, § 72(b) says that "Gross income does not include" a portion of each payment. In terms of § 72, the $100,000 is your Investment in the Contract, and your Expected Return is the $150,000. Multiply each payment by the ratio of Investment in the Contract to Expected Return, and exclude the result.

Here's how it works with the facts given:

$$\frac{\text{Investment in the contract} \quad \$100,000}{\text{Expected return} \qquad\qquad \$150,000} \quad \times \quad \$3,000 \quad = \quad \$2,000$$

So, each time a $3,000 annuity payment is received, $2,000 will be excluded, leaving $1,000 taxable. If you indeed receive exactly 50 payments, then an aggregate $100,000 will be excluded, and $50,000 will be taxable. It works out perfectly.

If you live longer than 50 years, § 72(b)(2) makes sure that you don't exclude any more than your $100,000 investment. On the other hand, if you live less than 50 years, § 72(b)(3) adjusts for that as well.

CHAPTER VII

Itemized Deductions

A. What Is an Itemized Deduction, and Why Does It Matter?

Generally speaking, business expenses should be deductible; personal expenditures should not. But some personal expenditures are deductible, anyway. However, if a personal expense is going to be deductible, it will probably have to be itemized. Itemized deductions are not treated as well as other deductions.

Have a look at the Tax Return in Chapter II. On Line 6, you enter your Total Income, and on Line 7, you enter your Adjusted Gross Income. Your business deductions (and any other deductions listed in Section 62) are the adjustments. You subtract them from Total Income to get to Adjusted Gross Income. You subtract them, no matter what.

On Line 8 of the Tax Return, you have a choice. You either enter the Standard Deduction, *or* you enter your Itemized Deductions. Not both. For a single taxpayer in 2018, the Standard Deduction is $12,000. So, if your actual Itemized Deductions exceed $12,000, then you itemize. If not, then you take the Standard Deduction. In the 2017 tax legislation, Congress made the Standard

Deduction much bigger than it was before. As a result, more people will take the Standard Deduction, and fewer people will itemize.

Itemizing makes the tax return more complicated. It requires more paperwork, because taxpayers have to be prepared to document their itemized expenses, such as medical expenses and charitable contributions. We Americans are not very good at keeping records to document our personal expenses. So, a larger Standard Deduction makes things simpler. However, it makes our tax laws less fair. It makes it less likely that certain extraordinary personal expenses, which may well affect a taxpayer's ability to pay taxes, are taken into account. You can decide for yourselves if the tradeoff is worth it.

Below, some of the more important itemized deductions will be addressed, in turn. The deduction for home mortgage interest is another highly significant itemized deduction. That deduction will be addressed with other interest deductions in Chapter VIII.

B. Medical Expenses

1. General

Imagine two taxpayers, Well and Sick, with equal adjusted 2019 gross incomes of $100,000. Well had no medical expenses. Sick, however, had three expensive operations, which cost her $60,000 out of pocket. If we stuck to the notion that personal expenses are nondeductible, then both Well and Sick would pay the same tax. However, Sick's ability to pay taxes is significantly lower than Well's, due to the extraordinary medical expenses. Therefore, Sick should get some adjustment to her tax bill.

That word "extraordinary" is crucial. Everyone has medical expenses, every year. We pay medical insurance premiums, and we have regular checkups, even if we are not sick. Needless to say, most of us have minor ailments, pretty much every year. So we don't want to allow a deduction for all medical expenses, only extraordinary ones.

When the medical expense deduction was first enacted in 1942, medical expenses in excess of 5% of adjusted gross income were deductible. That five per cent threshold was chosen because, at the time, the average American family spent 5% of adjusted gross income on medical expenses. By making that the threshold, Congress was allowing a deduction for above average medical expenses. In 1954, based upon some evidence that the average American family spent only 3% of adjusted gross income on medical care, the threshold was lowered to 3%.

Since then, two things happened. The first was that medical expenses started going up, with the average American family spending considerably more than 3% of AGI per year on medical care. The second was that the IRS did some studies of which lines of the 1040 tax return form and its schedules led to the most mistakes, and discovered that the lines for medical expenses and casualty losses were the winners. Of course, these could have been honest mistakes, or, uh, cheating. Congress and the IRS decided that, if the thresholds for these deductions were raised, then fewer people would get to take them, and fewer, uh, mistakes would be made. As a result, the threshold for medical expenses is now up to 10% of AGI (7.5% of AGI for 2017 and 2018). That means that, in the example above, Sick would be able to deduct the amount by which her medical expenses exceeded 10% or her AGI.

Medical expenses	$60,000
- 10% of AGI	$10,000
Deductible medical expense	$50,000

Section 213 is a hardship deduction. It assumes that your medical expenses were beyond your control. If you choose to incur medical expenses, that's not a hardship. Therefore, cosmetic surgery is defined out of "medical care" by § 213(d)(9), "unless the surgery or procedure is necessary to ameliorate a deformity arising from, or directly related to, a congenital abnormality, a personal injury resulting from an accident or trauma, or disfiguring disease."

Cosmetic surgery is itself defined in § 213(d)(9)(B) as:

Any procedure which is directed at improving the patient's appearance and does not meaningfully promote the proper function of the body or prevent or treat illness or disease.

So what about a sex change operation? The deductibility of those medical expenses was in doubt, but in the recent case of O'Donnabhain v. Commissioner, 134 T.C. 34 (2010), the hormone therapy and sex reassignment surgery expenses were deductible, but the breast augmentation surgery expenses were not.

2. *Medical Travel*

In Commissioner v. Bilder, 369 U.S. 499 (1962), the taxpayer was advised by his doctor to move to Florida, for legitimate medical reasons. Accordingly, the taxpayer sought to deduct all of his post-move living expenses. The Supreme Court said no. They held that the expenses of *getting* to a place of medical care were deductible, but the expenses of *being* at the new location were not.

Congress modified *Bilder*, in part, by enacting § 213(d)(2):

Amounts paid for certain lodging away from home treated as paid for medical care.—Amounts paid for lodging (not lavish or extravagant under the circumstances) while away from home primarily for and essential to medical care . . .shall be treated as amounts paid for medical care if—

(A) The medical care . . . is provided by a physical in a licensed hospital (or in a medical care facility which is related to, or the equivalent of, a licensed hospital), and

(B) There is no significant element of personal pleasure, recreation, or vacation in the travel away from home.

The amount taken into account under the preceding sentence shall not exceed $50 for each night for such individual.

So, if you travel to Rochester, Minnesota, to undergo surgery at the Mayo Clinic on an outpatient basis, and stay in a motel across the street from the Clinic, your lodging expenses will be deemed deductible medical expenses, to the extent of $50 per night. Luckily, it is hard to imagine any significant amount of personal pleasure, recreation, or vacation in a trip to Rochester, Minnesota.

C. Casualty Losses

Imagine two taxpayers, Lucky and Unlucky, with identical Adjusted Gross Incomes of $100,000. Lucky has no personal casualty losses, but Unlucky had a car wreck and a house fire this year, with losses in excess of insurance of $25,000. Surely, Unlucky has less ability to pay taxes than Lucky. For most of our tax history, personal casualty losses in excess of 10% of AGI were Itemized Deductions. However, the 2017 Tax Cuts and Jobs Act severely limited the casualty loss deduction. From now until 2025, only those personal casualties attributable to a Presidentially declared disaster will be recognized.

D. Charitable Contributions

Unlike medical expenses and casualty losses, the charitable contribution deduction is not justified by extraordinary hardship. Rather, it is justified because we, as a society, like to encourage charitable giving. Moreover, the government likes contributions to charity because sometimes, charities end up doing things that the government might have done—perhaps in the area of welfare or educational expenses. Thus, charities can save the government money.

1. What Is a Charitable Contribution?

Charitable contributions have much in common with gifts. In both cases, one would not expect there to be a quid pro quo. In fact, if there is a partial quid pro quo, then the value of what is received back to the donor is subtracted from the deductible contribution. If you contribute to your local public radio station, and they give you a tote bag, the value of the tote bag is subtracted from the value of your contribution. And it's up to the radio station to tell you what the tote bag was worth.

2. Who Is a Charitable Donee?

Charitable donees are described in § 170(c), but not very helpfully. At least, § 170(c) does tell us no part of the net earnings of the charitable donee can inure to the benefit of any private citizen. Section 170(b)(1)(A) gives us a better sense of things. Right off the top, in subsections (i), (ii), and (iii), it mentions churches, schools and hospitals. That's a start, anyway.

Section 170(b) tells us that charitable donees come in two flavors—public, as described in § 170(b)(1)(A), and private, described in § 170(b)(1)(B). Public charities include the churches, schools and hospitals mentioned above. In fact, deductible charitable organizations include a bewildering array of institutions, including, for example, the Save Your Ass Foundation, dedicated to the prevention of cruelty to wild donkeys. Private charitable donees are any charitable donees which are not public. Generally, they are established by individual donors, who then have a fair amount of say in managing them.

3. *Mechanics*

Let's get back to those two flavors—public and private. There are ceilings on charitable donations. The ceilings are determined with reference to "contribution base," which is essentially adjusted gross income. Okay, if you must know, it is AGI without net operating loss carrybacks. See § 170(b)(1)(G).

Contributions to public charities are considered first, then contributions to private charities. Contributions of cash to public charities are deductible up to 60% of your contribution base. Noncash contributions to public charities are capped at 50% of AGI. Contributions to private charities are limited to the lesser of 30% of your contribution base in the taxable year, or the excess of 50% of your contribution base over the amount of your contributions to public charities. Then there are some special rules for contributions of appreciated property. Amounts in excess of these limits can be carried forward to succeeding years.

Say your contribution base is $200,000. Say the only contributions you made this year were $125,000 in cash to public charities. If so, $120,000 (60% of your contribution base) will be deductible this year. The rest is carried over to next year.

Say the only contributions you made this year were $125,000 to private charities. You will be allowed to deduct $60,000 of them this year (30% of your contribution base). The rest will be carried over.

Say you gave $90,000 in cash to public charities, and $50,000 to private charities. The $90,000 to public charities is deductible off the top. As to that $50,000 contribution to private charities, you get to deduct the lesser of $60,000 or $10,000. The $60,000 is 30% of your contribution base. The $10,000 is:

50% of your contribution base	$100,000
– contributions to public charities	<u>-$90,000</u>
Excess	$10,000

Ten thousand is less than sixty thousand, so you get to deduct $10,000. The rest carries over.

Now let's talk about appreciated property. Say you have an asset with a zero basis, worth $125,000. If you sold it, you'd have to pay tax on the gain of $125,000. So, you think, you'll donate it to charity, and get a deduction for the fair market value of the contributed asset—or $125,000.

Congress says that's too much of a good thing—avoiding the tax on the gain and getting a deduction, besides. As a result, they enacted § 170(e). Capital gains are taxed favorably, while ordinary gains are not. See Chapter X. Therefore, avoiding capital gains by contributing the appreciated asset is not so damaging to the federal fisc as avoiding ordinary income. So, § 170(e) distinguishes between "capital gain property" (property which, if sold, would be taxed at favorable capital gains rates) and "ordinary income property" (property which, if sold, would be taxed at ordinary income rates).

Ordinary income is relatively simple. Let's say that your asset was not a capital asset. If you had sold it, you would have been taxed on ordinary gain of $125,000. If you contribute it to charity, section 170(e)(1)(A) says that your charitable contribution deduction will be the amount otherwise allowed (the fair market value of the property at the time of the contribution) minus any gain that would have ordinary gain had you sold the property.

So, your deduction will be:

Otherwise allowable deduction (fmv of property)	$125,000
– Ordinary gain	$125,000
Allowable charitable deduction	$0

What if, instead, the property was capital asset? Assume that, if you had sold it, the gain would have been $125,000 of long term capital gain. Once again, the otherwise allowable deduction would have been the fair market value of the contributed property, or $125,000. This time, however, since it's capital gain property, you look to § 170(e)(1)(B). According to § 170(e)(1)(B)(i)(I), if the property is:

- tangible
- personal
- put to an unrelated use,

then you will subtract the capital appreciation from your deduction.

"Tangible" you know. A gold bar is tangible. Goodwill is not. "Personal" means it's not real estate.

Let's look more closely at unrelated use. The statute says:

. . . if the use by the donee is unrelated to the purpose or function constituting the basis for its exemption under section 501.

Section 501 is the section that allows certain organizations to be tax exempt. Art museums, for example, are tax exempt because they provide public access to great works of art. Hospitals are exempt because they provide medical care.

Let's say that you owned a painting, with a basis of $0 and a current fair market value of $125,000. You propose to donate it to a hospital. The hospital plans to sell the painting. Selling the painting is not using it for the hospital's exempt purpose. Therefore, the painting is tangible, it is personal, and the use by the donee is unrelated to its exempt function. The $125,000 of capital gain will be subtracted from the otherwise allowable deduction. Thus:

Otherwise allowable deduction (fmv of property)	$125,000
– Charitable gain	$125,000
Allowable charitable deduction	$0

Now let's say that you donated that painting to an art museum, which plans to display it. The painting is tangible, and it is personal, but now the use is *not* unrelated to the art museum's exempt function. Therefore, not all of the requirements of § 170(e)(1)(B)(i) are met, so the capital gains are not subtracted. The allowable deduction is the full fair market value of $125,000.

Not so fast. Under § 170(b)(1)(C), you have a choice. If you go with the result described above, with a full $125,000 deduction, you are subject to a special cap of 30% of your contribution base. If your contribution base is still $200,000, that cap is $60,000. The excess over that cap can be carried over until next year.

However, you can make an election under § 170(b)(12)(C)(iii). If you do so, there will be no 30% cap, but you will subtract the $125,000 of capital gain from your allowable deduction. Your choice.

4.   *Unrelated Business Income Tax*

In 1947, the Mueller Macaroni Company was donated to New York University. After that, NYU, a tax exempt, educational institution, sold noodles in competition with other, tax-paying macaroni companies. That's not fair.

In response, Congress enacted the Unrelated Business Income Tax—Internal Revenue Code starting at Section 511. It provides, generally speaking, that, if a tax-exempt institution generates income which is unrelated to its exempt function, then that institution will pay taxes on that income, just like anybody else. Therefore, NYU would have to pay tax on its noodle income, even though it would still be tax-exempt with respect to any income relating to its educational function.

So far, so good. But what income is related to an institution's exempt function? Christmas card sales from art museum gift shops are tax exempt, related to the exempt function of the art museum, even though such sales are a very substantial business, in direct competition with tax paying card shops.

Here are two stories. At least one of them is real.

Story #1. Synagogues traditionally take some time during Yom Kippur services to solicit donations from the congregation for the good of the temple. At one such solicitation, a member rose, and said:

> You all know me. I own the butcher shop on Main Street. We sell the finest kosher meats. This week we're having a sale on lamb chops. We are open Mondays through Thursdays. I would like to contribute $100, anonymously.

Story #2. The Cotton Bowl is one of the nation's oldest college football bowl games. It has enjoyed many different sponsorship arrangements over the years. In 1991, Mobil Oil donated over $1,000,000 to the Cotton Bowl Association, which was a tax-exempt organization. In return, a number of good things happened to Mobil Oil:

- The game was renamed the Mobil Oil Cotton Bowl;

- The players' uniforms had the words "Mobil Oil" written on them;

- "Mobil Oil" was mentioned at least four times during the broadcasts; and

- The words "Mobil Oil" were prominently displayed on both end zones, as you can see.

As to Story #1: was the donor really donating the $100, or was he buying advertising?

As to Story #2: same question. In addition, when the Cotton Bowl Association accepted the $1,000,000, did they have income related to their exempt function, or were they earning income from the unrelated business of advertising?

In the Mobil Oil Cotton Bowl, IRS opined that the Cotton Bowl Association had taxable UBIT income. However, the political pressure was so great that IRS had to retract. But see § 513(i).

E. State and Local Taxes

We Americans don't only pay federal income taxes. Depending upon where we live, we might also pay state and local income taxes, state and local sales taxes, federal estate and gift taxes, local gift and inheritance taxes, state property taxes, and excise taxes, just to name a few. Bummer. Some of these other taxes might be, or might appear to be, double or triple taxes on the same thing. Some folks might be a tad less enthusiastic about paying state and local taxes if they feel that the feds have already taxed them on the same thing. Perhaps for this reason, state and local taxes (SALT) are an itemized deduction against your federal income.

However, the 2017 Tax Cuts and Jobs Act capped the SALT deductions (other than those taxes attributable to business) at $10,000, from now until 2025.

SALT deductions have different impacts on different states. Some states, like New York, levy high taxes on their citizens. Others, like Mississippi, tax their citizens at a much lower rate. Therefore, a cap on SALT deductions hurts the high-tax states disproportionately. Once again, the increased standard deduction alleviates some of the pain of the SALT cap. However, the increased standard deduction does nothing to alleviate the special pain of New Yorkers, vs. Mississippians. Then again, some of the fine folks in Mississippi might well ask why anyone in his or her right mind would care to live in New York, and some of the fine folks in New York might well ask why anyone in his or her right mind would care to live in Mississippi.

CHAPTER VIII

Mixed Motive Expenses

Business expenses are easy. They're deductible. Personal expenses are pretty easy. They're nondeductible, except for the special cases described in Chapter VII. But what about mixed motive expenses?

A. Huge Caveat

Many mixed motive expenses are incurred by employees. For example, imagine an employee on a business trip. She incurs expenses for transportation, meals and lodging while away from home on business. If her employer reimburses her, no problem. After the reimbursement, she is not out of pocket for the trip, so she can't deduct. However, if she pays for the trip, then one would think that she could deduct her expenses.

For most of our tax history, such unreimbursed employee business expenses were deductible, at least in part. However, from now until the end of 2025, they are not deductible at all. Therefore, when you consider the expenses described in this chapter, especially travel expenses and clothing expenses, remember that, until 2025, they might be deductible by self-employed persons, but not by employees.

B. Travel Expenses

Travel expenses are mostly for meals and lodging. Meals and lodging are the quintessential personal expenses. You weren't allowed to deduct your meals and lodging expenses while you were home; why should you be allowed to deduct them just because you are away from home on business? The idea is that you should be allowed to deduct these away-from-home expenses because they are greater than they would have been, had you stayed home. As to lodging expenses, they are often duplicative. Even when you are away on business in L.A., you still pay rent on your apartment in New York.

For meal expenses, they are not duplicative—you are not eating twice—but they are probably more expensive on the road. Had you stayed home, you might have brought a sandwich to work with you. You might even have gone home for lunch. When you're a plane trip away, those cheaper options are not there; you have no choice but to have your meal at a restaurant. So, the meals and lodging expenses, which otherwise would have been nondeductible personal expenses, become deductible because the business trip makes them more expensive.

Why does the statute say that your business travel expenses can't be lavish or extravagant? Because, although the reason for the trip to L.A. might have been purely business, your choice of the penthouse suite at the Beverly Hilton was not.

Some things we know. Commuting expenses are nondeductible. Why? Because we consider it to be your choice whether you live close to work or far from work.

How about really short trips? United States v. Correll, 389 U.S. 299 (1967) gave us the "overnight" rule. Say you leave New York in the morning for a business meeting in Philadelphia. You have lunch in Philadelphia, go to your meeting, and return home to New York that evening. Is the lunch deductible? No, because you were not away from home overnight.

On the other hand, if you fly from New York to L.A. for a week on business, then all of your meals in LA are deductible (At least in part. See below), because you are away from home overnight. What about long distance truckers, and night owls? For them, and anyone else, the "overnight" rule morphs into the "sleep or rest" rule. If you are away from home long enough to require sleep or rest away from home before you get back, that satisfies the "overnight" rule.

What about longer trips? Here's one way of looking at it. If you go away from home on a business trip that is so long that any reasonable person would have pulled up stakes and moved—i.e. sell your house, terminate your lease—then your away-from-home expenses are nondeductible. Even if you didn't move, you should have. On the other hand, if the trip is so short that you would have been crazy to pull up stakes and move, then the expenses of the trip should be deductible.

Where do we draw the line? Congress has drawn the line at one year. But they did it in a somewhat confusing way. Section 162(a)(2) allows the traveling expenses, but after § 162(a)(3), in the middle of the next paragraph, it says

> For purposes of paragraph (2), the taxpayer shall not be treated as being temporarily away from home during any period of employment if such period exceeds 1 year.

Imagine that you go on a business trip which you reasonably expect will take 18 months. However, you manage to wrap things up more quickly than you expect, so you return home in 10 months.

The statutory language just quoted asks if ". . .such period exceeds 1 year." When do you know how long "such period" was? You wait until after the period is over, and then you see how long it was. So, because the trip in fact was less than 1 year, your travel expenses should have been nondeductible.

But when is it that you have to decide either to pull up stakes and move, or not? You don't make that decision after the trip; you make it before the trip. In this case, before the trip, you reasonably expected that the trip would last more than a year. Therefore, from this perspective, the trip was too long, and the expenses should have been nondeductible.

The statute appears to ask how long the trip actually was. However, the IRS, in Revenue Ruling 93-86, asks instead how long you "reasonably expected" the trip to be. I think the IRS has the better view. But how can the IRS take that position, in light of the statutory language?

Let's go back to meals for a moment. Originally, the deductions for meals eaten while away from home on business were limited to the excess of the cost of the meal away from home over what one would have spent at home. Thus, if at home one would have eaten a peanut butter and jelly sandwich, at a cost of, say fifty cents, but one had lunch in a restaurant while away from home on business at a cost of, say, $10.00, then the deductible portion of the meal would have been the excess expense of $9.50. However, by as early as 1921, we realized that we were asking for people to make an impossible calculation. So, instead, we gave up, and ruled that the entire meal, not just the excess, would be deductible.

Much later, Congress enacted § 274(n), which limits the meal and entertainment expenses to 50% of their cost. More recently, the Tax Cuts and Jobs Act provided that such meals may not be lavish or extravagant, either. Anyway, why 50%? Perhaps a deduction of 50% is a quick and easy way of deducting only the excess cost.

Note that we are talking merely of unreimbursed meals while away from home on business. We are assuming that you don't do anything during the meal but eat—presumably alone. If, however, you have a business lunch, perhaps with clients, that's a different story altogether.

Now, what about a trip when you really do some business things and some personal things? Suppose, for example, that you leave Duluth, Minnesota in February to go on a three day business trip to Miami—Monday through Wednesday—but you decide to stay until Friday night to relax on the beach. Is the trip business or personal? Regulation § 1.162-2(b)(1) says that the expenses of getting there are treated one way, while the expenses incurred while there are treated in another. As to getting there, it's all or nothing. If the trip was primarily business, the costs of getting there (usually airfare) are fully deductible. If the trip was primarily personal, then the costs of getting there are fully nondeductible. How do you tell? Time spent. In the example given, if you spend 3 of the 5 days on business, then the trip is primarily business. Anything more than 50% is primarily business.

The costs of being there, however, can be allocated. In the example listed above, the trip was primarily business, so the airfare is deductible. However, once there, only the expenses incurred on Monday, Tuesday and Wednesday, are deductible. Those were the business days. The expenses incurred on Thursday and Friday are personal and nondeductible.

Some of these mixed motive expenses have been subject to a fair amount of taxpayer abuse. To address some of the more problematic areas, Congress enacted § 274. Subsection (d), for example, provides that traveling expenses are not deductible unless they are substantiated in detail. Regulation § 1.274-5T suggests that it is far better if the substantiation is contemporaneous with the travel, rather than being after the fact. If old fashioned expense diaries are kept, rather than the more modern laptop entries, care should be taken with the color of ink used. If all entries are made in the same color ink, they will look like they have been done after the fact. You don't want to do that. Different colors are better. For that matter, a ketchup stain or two would not be a bad idea. I'm just saying.

C. Clothing

The rule is simple. If you are required to wear specific items of clothing for work, they are deductible if, and only if, you could not have worn that clothing after work. This rule, as explained by Pevsner v. Commissioner, 628 F.2d 467 (5th Cir. 1980), is objective, not subjective. Mrs. Pevsner, a saleswoman for Yves St Laurent, was required to wear YSL clothing at work. She explained, convincingly, I thought, that the YSL clothing was not compatible with her lifestyle. Therefore, even though she could have worn it at home, she didn't. The court denied her deduction, holding that it would be too difficult to consider all of the myriad personal variables. If, as an objective matter, one could have worn the clothing outside work, then the clothing expenses are nondeductible, even if one didn't wear the clothing outside of work.

Under current law, Mrs. Pevsner would have been totally out of luck, because she was an employee. Until 2025, business expenses of employees are nondeductible.

ABBA furnishes a good example of the clothing rule. Presumably, the Swedish tax law was similar to ours, in this respect. Apparently, their tax counsel told them to wear outrageous outfits, impossible to be worn at home, in order to ensure deductibility. They did.

Don't try this on at home.

D. Meals and Entertainment with Clients

Say you take your client to lunch, whether at home or away. That's different from the travel expenses described above. Now, as long as you discuss business, either during the meal or reasonably soon before or after, that's deductible. A doctor friend of mine tells of having lunch with his doctor friends. At some point during the lunch, one of them asks the others, "How's business?"

"Fine," they say. They all pause for a moment to make a note in their laptops that they are having a deductible business lunch. Then, they go back to talking about sports.

Entertainment that was directly related to the taxpayer's business activities used to be partially deductible. Now, it is not deductible at all.

E. Education

1. In General

Education seems like the quintessential personal expense. But what if you obtain the education in order to improve your business? Now that's different. But, arguably, isn't all education likely to help you to earn money, somehow?

The regulations have two positive rules, and two negative rules, on business deductions for education. Here are the two negative ones. Educational expenses are *nondeductible* if they:

- Are required to meet the minimum educational requirements for qualification in employment or other trade or business. Reg. § 1.162-5(b)(2). So much for law school tuition;

- Will lead to qualifying in a new trade or business. Reg. § 1.162-5(b)(3).

Now here are the two positive rules. Educational expenditures are *deductible* if they:

- Maintain or improve skills required by the business. Reg. § 1.162-5(a)(1); or

- Meet the express requirements of the employer, or the requirements of applicable law or regulations, imposed as a condition to the retention of the employment relationship. Reg. § 1.162-5(a)(2).

That second rule is of doubtful utility, since, from now until 2025, employee business expenses will be nondeductible.

One of the trickiest parts is to determine when you qualify for a new trade or business. For example, going from elementary school teacher to high school teacher is not qualifying for a new trade or business, nor is going from classroom teacher to principal. Many other examples come to mind. Most of them have been resolved, either in the regulations, or in the revenue rulings.

Here's some exciting news. Practicing tax law is not different enough from practicing general law to be a new trade or business. Getting an LL.M. in tax, therefore, might be deductible. But timing is important. If you go right from your three years of J.D. law school to your one year of Tax LL.M., before you go into practice, then the LL.M. degree appears to be just like the law degree, meeting what were for you the minimum educational requirements of your job. What's more, you would have incurred the LLM expenses before you were "carrying on" a business, so you would lose under Section 162. However, if you practice law for some substantial period, and then go back to get a Tax LL.M. degree, then it looks like maintaining or improving skills—fully deductible.

But wait! There's more! Typically, an LL.M. degree takes an academic year, which is a bit less than twelve months. So, if you go away from home for, say, ten months to get an LL.M., then you're away from home on business for less than a year. You get to deduct not only your books and tuition, but also your meals and lodging. Sweet.

Remember, however, that no deduction is allowable for the business education expenses of an employee. So, if you are a solo practitioner, you might be able to deduct your LLM, and your CLE expenses. However, if you are an associate in a law firm, these expenses will be nondeductible.

2. *Tax Incentives for Education*

There are quite a few. They include the Hope Scholarship Credit, § 25A(b), and the Lifetime Learning Credit, § 25A(c). Note that both of these are credits, not deductions. They also phase down for higher incomes. There is also the deduction for interest on education loans, § 221, which also phases down for higher incomes, and § 529 plans, which allow parents, and others, to save, taxfree, for their children's education. This stuff can be really important to you. If you want the details, have a look at IRS Publication 970—Tax Benefits for Education. This IRS Publication does a good job of walking you through the benefits, and it's free!

While you're at it, you might consider whether all of these tax benefits actually do benefit the students, or whether they are, in fact, merely an excuse for institutions of higher education to raise tuition.

F. The Home Office Deduction

Back in the dark ages, most family doctors had their offices in their homes. As often as not, there would be two doors, and two doorbells. One was for the residence, and the other was for the doctor's office. Surely, such doctors should have been allowed to deduct the costs of that portion of their homes used for their business, and they were.

But other people abused it. Stick a laptop in your bedroom closet, and voilà! A portion of your home is now your office, and a portion of your home expenses are now deductible.

Congress reacted to that scam by enacting the current § 280A. The general rule of § 280A(a) provides:

> In the case of a taxpayer who is an individual or an S corporation, no deduction otherwise allowable under this chapter shall be allowed with respect to the use of a dwelling unit which is used by the taxpayer during the taxable year as a residence.

But there are exceptions. Subsection 280A(c) provides that you can deduct a portion of the dwelling unit which is **exclusively used** on a regular basis—

(A) As the principal place of business for any trade or business of the taxpayer,

(B) As a place of business which is used by patients, clients or customers in meeting or dealing with the taxpayer in the normal course of his trade or business, or

(C) In the case of a separate structure which is not attached to the dwelling unit, in connecting with the taxpayer's trade or business.

The language after (C) has an important caveat:

For purposes of Paragraph A, the term "principal place of business" includes a place of business which is used by the taxpayer for the administrative or management activities of any trade or business of the taxpayer if there is no other fixed location of such trade or business where the taxpayer conducts substantial administrative or managements activities of such trade or business.

This last excerpt was enacted in response to Commissioner v. Soliman, 506 U.S. 168 (1993). Dr. Soliman was an anesthesiologist, who worked mostly in hospitals. However, he had paperwork responsibilities. Since none of his employers provided him with office space in which to do the paperwork, he did it at home. The Supreme Court held that his "principal place of business, under § 280A(c)(1), was determined by considering the relative importance of the activities, and the time spent. It found that what he did in the hospital was more important than the paperwork he did at home. Further, he spent more time in the hospital than he did on the paperwork at home. Therefore, they denied Dr. Soliman his home office deduction. As you can see, Congress added language to ensure that future taxpayers in Dr. Soliman's situation would be allowed to deduct their home office expenses.

Remember, of course, that today Mr. Soliman would be out of luck, because he is an employee.

G. Child Care

Say you have a job and you have a child. But for the job, you wouldn't have the child care expenses. That looks business. And yet, but for the child, you wouldn't have the child care expenses. That looks personal.

Not surprisingly, Congress compromised. Yes, there is a credit for child care expenses, but let's look at all of the decisions they made.

First, § 21 is a credit. That means that it is worth the same to a high income taxpayer or a low income taxpayer. But maybe not. The amount of the credit phases down as your income goes up. For low income taxpayers, the credit is 35% of employment-related household and dependent care expenses. However, that 35% phases down by 1 percentage point for each $2,000, or fraction of $2,000, by which the taxpayer's adjusted gross income exceeds $15,000. But the percentage plateaus at 20%. So, making it a credit suggests that income level doesn't matter, but then they phase down the percentage for higher incomes, suggesting that income level does matter.

Second, the credit maxes out at two children. In § 21(c), we find that the creditable amount is capped at $3,000 for one qualifying individual, and $6,000 for *two or more* qualifying individuals. Thus, if you have two children, or if you have ten children, the cap is still $6,000. Apparently, Congress thinks that two kids are plenty.

Third, the employment-related expenses cannot exceed earned income. See § 21(d). If the taxpayer is married, then the employment-related expenses cannot exceed the income of the lesser earning spouse. So far, that means that, if one spouse stays at home and earns no income, then there can be no employment-related expenses, hence no child care credit. Further, one cannot use the child care credit to allow one to do volunteer work, which, of course, leads to zero earned income. This result is also dictated by the fact that employment-related expenses are defined in § 21(b)(2) as expenses designed to keep one gainfully employed.

If one spouse works outside the home, and the other is a full time student, then it would seem that there would be no child care credit, since the student spouse would earn little or no income. However, § 21(d)(2) provides that, in that situation, the student spouse will be deemed to have earned income for each month of full-time student status of:

- $250 if there is one qualifying child, or

- $500 if there are two or more qualifying children.

Accordingly, if the spouse were a full-time student for nine months of the year with two children, that spouse would be deemed to have earned $4,500 for the purposes of the section 21(d) limitation. Once more, note that the benefit is capped at two children.

Finally, employment related expenses do not include the expenses of sending a child to overnight camp. See § 21(b)(2). Why not? Is this something that only rich people do?

H. Bad Debts

Businesses loan money. Sometimes, they don't get it back. Of course, bad debts should be a legitimate business deduction.

However, it would be tempting to disguise nonbusiness situations as business situations, in order to obtain an undeserved deduction. What if, for example, Father transfers money to Son as a gift, and claims that the transfer was a business loan, which went bad. We need a way to argue that the transfer either wasn't a loan in the first place, or, if it was, it was not a business loan.

Section 166 distinguishes business loans from nonbusiness loans. There are two consequences to the distinction. First, a business bad debt can be deducted when it is only partially worthless. A nonbusiness bad debt can only be deducted when it is totally worthless.

Second, a totally worthless nonbusiness bad debt is treated as a short term capital loss. Therefore, it must first be netted out against capital gains, and, if there is an excess loss, it can only be deducted at the rate of $3,000 per year, with the rest carried over. See Chapter X. Business bad debts, in contrast, are deductible as ordinary deductions. Trust me—ordinary deductions are better.

The Supreme Court, in United States v. Generes, 405 U.S. 1033 (1972), gives helpful guidance on the nature of business bad debts. In *Generes*, the taxpayer was an employee in his son's business, and also an investor in the son's business. He loaned money to his son, to protect his job, and his investment. Protecting his job was a business loan; protecting his investment was not. Which one was it? The Supreme Court held that the proper inquiry was to determine the lender's dominant motivation for the loan. In this case, the amount of the investment was far greater than the amount of the employment earnings, so protecting the investment was the dominant motivation. The business bad debt deduction was denied.

Note that, under current law, the deduction would have been denied even if the court had found that the dominant motivation had been to protect the job. In that event, the expense would have been related to the taxpayer's employment, and therefore still nondeductible.

I. Interest

1. *General*

Businesses often have to borrow money, and pay interest on their debt. Of course, that interest should be deductible. And it is— mostly. It should be equally obvious that the interest on personal loans—say a vacation trip—should be nondeductible. But how do you tell the difference?

Say I have $10,000 in the bank, and I borrow another $10,000. I incur two expenses—a $10,000 ordinary business expense, and a $10,000 personal vacation. If I use the $10,000 in the bank for my business expense and the $10,000 in loan proceeds on the vacation, then the loan was a personal loan, and the interest is nondeductible. So, I won't do that. Instead, I use the money in the bank for the vacation, and I use the loan proceeds for the business expense. Now the interest is deductible. How, in real life, can the government trace the fungible loan proceeds, and prove that I used them one way or the other?

They can't. That's why, for most of our history, they gave up, and declared that all interest was deductible. That means that significant personal expenses, which should not be deductible, will be deducted anyway. The biggest of these is the interest on your personal home mortgage. Over the years, there have been a number of attempts to abolish the deduction for personal home mortgage interest. But, when so many voters enjoy a deduction, it becomes very hard to get rid of it.

Finally, in 1986, we reached a bit of a compromise, or, if you like, we caved. Now, personal interest is nondeductible, **except** for home mortgage interest. And what is home mortgage interest? It is interest on a loan secured by your personal home. It does not matter what you do with the loan proceeds. Therefore, if you bought your house for $500,000 cash, and your house is still worth $500,000, you can borrow any amount up to $500,000, using the house as collateral, and then use those loan proceeds to go on vacation. The interest will still be deductible.

There is, however, a new wrinkle. Before the 1917 Tax Cuts and Jobs Act, one could deduct home mortgage interest if it was "acquisition indebtedness" or if it was "home equity indebtedness." You incur acquisition indebtedness if you borrow money to buy, build, or improve the residence. That is still deductible, within limits. You incur home equity indebtedness if you borrow money, using the home as collateral, and spend it on anything else. That is no longer deductible.

Let's say that you buy a house for $200,000, paying $50,000 down and borrowing the remaining $150,000. That $150,000 loan is acquisition indebtedness, and the interest on that loan will be deductible.

Imagine that the house goes up in value to $275,000. You take a second mortgage on the house for $25,000, and go on vacation. That $25,000 would be home equity indebtedness. Interest on that debt used to be deductible, but no more.

2.   *Low Interest and No Interest Loans*

Father wants to give Son the use of a million dollars, but Father doesn't want to give it to Son outright. So Father loans the money to Son. If Father charged market interest rates, then the interest payments—say $50,000 per year—would be taxable to Father at his high marginal rates. So, Father loans the money to Son at zero interest. Now, when Son uses the money to earn income, the income will be taxable to Son, at Son's relatively low marginal rates.

Congress, in § 7872, has shut down this scheme. In such a transaction, Father will be deemed, for tax purposes, to have charged Son the interest he should have charged. Further, Father will be deemed to have made a separate transfer to Son of the amount of that interest. Now, having made these two presumptions, the chips will fall where they may.

In the Father-Son scenario, it works like this.

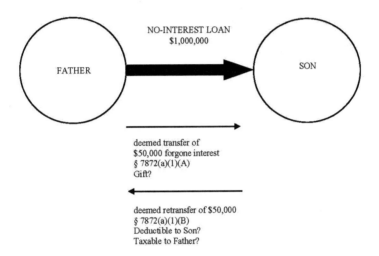

Why would Father have given $50,000 per year to Son? It looks like a gift, nondeductible to Father, taxfree to Son. What about the deemed payments of $50,000 back from Son to Father? From Son's standpoint, it's deductible interest if and only if the loan was a business loan, or a home mortgage loan. From Father's standpoint, it looks like taxable interest, either way.

How about an Employer-Employee scenario?

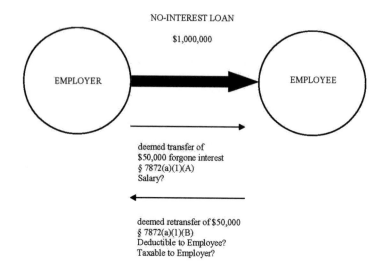

NO-INTEREST LOAN

$1,000,000

EMPLOYER

EMPLOYEE

deemed transfer of
$50,000 forgone interest
§ 7872(a)(1)(A)
Salary?

deemed retransfer of $50,000
§ 7872(a)(1)(B)
Deductible to Employee?
Taxable to Employer?

Why would Employer give $50,000 per year to Employee? It looks like salary, deductible to Employer, taxable to Employee. Why would Employee give the $50,000 per year back? From the employee's standpoint, it is interest—deductible or not, depending on the nature of the loan. From the Employer's standpoint, it is taxable. In this case, notice that, if the deemed interest turns out to be deductible to the Employee, then the transaction is a wash for both parties.

CHAPTER IX

Timing

Would you rather pay your taxes this year or next year? Duh. Of course, you can always pay your taxes late, and the IRS will be happy to charge you interest, and maybe penalties. Not a great idea. But if you can defer the *taxable event* until next year, then you're really much better off. Now, you're not paying your taxes late, and the IRS can't charge you interest or penalties.

Actually, it might be even better than that. Say I'm 64 years old, planning to retire at 65. Right now, I'm in my peak earning years. Next year, my income will go down considerably, when I retire. If you tax me on an item of income this year, before I retire, it will be taxed at relatively high marginal rates. However, if I could defer that income until next year, it will be taxed at considerably lower marginal rates. Good deal.

Now, remember the basic arithmetic. There's income, and deductions. You want to recognize income as late as possible. On the other hand, you want to take deductions as early as possible, because deductions reduce taxable income. That's what timing is about. Actually, we've already talked about the timing of deductions a bit. The whole issue with respect to capital expenses vs. ordinary deductions (See Chapter VI) is, essentially, a question of whether you want to take all of your deductions right now, or whether you'll have to spread them out. That's timing.

In fact, some say that, in 1986, when Congress and the IRS shut down as many tax schemes as they could, it turned out that timing was one of the last ones left. Timing is in part a question of how you do your accounting, and in part a question of how you arrange things. Let's talk about accounting first. Bear with me. It's not as bad as you think.

A. Accounting Methods

Basically, accounting methods come in two flavors—cash and accrual. Cash is probably what you are used to. On the cash method, you recognize income when the cash hits your pocket, and you take a deduction when the cash leaves your pocket. Accrual is a bit different. You accrue income when you know that you have a right to it, and when you know exactly how much it is. You accrue a deduction when you know that you owe the money, and you know exactly how much you owe.

Let's take a common situation. Lawyer agrees to do legal work for $100. Lawyer does the legal work in Year 1, and sends Client a bill for $100. Client is completely satisfied with the work. Client pays the bill in Year 2.

From the Lawyer's perspective, on the cash method of accounting, she has income in Year 2, when she was actually paid. On the accrual method, she has income in Year 1, because that's when she knew that she had an absolute right to the money, and she knew how much money it was.

Let's look at the Client's perspective. Assume that the legal fees were deductible as a business expenses. If Client were on the cash basis, the fee would be deductible in Year 2, when she paid it.

If she were on the accrual basis, it would be deductible in Year 1, when she owed it.

Now, a few wrinkles. On the cash basis of accounting, you have income when you receive the *cash*, or the *cash equivalent*. That means that you have cash income when you receive cash, a check, or a credit card payment. You also have cash income when you receive property or services. So, for example, if the Client gave the lawyer a camera worth $100 in payment for legal services, then the cash basis Lawyer recognizes the taxable income when he receives the camera. If the Client pays the Lawyer by doing $100 worth of house painting, then the $100 is recognizable income when the house painting is complete.

What if Client comes to Lawyer on December 31, Year 1, with $100 cash in hand, ready to pay his bill. Lawyer says, "For tax reasons, I'd rather recognize this income next year. Please hold on to the $100 and pay me in January." Does this work? No. The cash basis Lawyer has *constructive receipt* of the $100 in December, because the money was set aside for her, and she could have accessed it without penalty. Nice try. See Regulation § 1.451-2.

Most large businesses are required to use the accrual basis of accounting. But, for those of us with a choice, which is better?

Let's talk about the way things really happen in America. You buy something today. You don't pay for it until tomorrow. What does that mean? Looking just at the "seller," for the income side of things, you would rather have taxable income later, not earlier. Therefore, you'll prefer the cash basis of accounting, because you usually earn the right to the income (and therefore accrue it) before you actually get paid.

Looking, however, at "buyer," for the deduction side of things, you would rather have a deduction earlier, not later. Therefore, you'll prefer the accrual basis of accounting, because you usually owe the money before you pay it.

Now, of course, all of us care about both income and deductions, so which accounting method do we prefer? Usually, it doesn't matter a whole lot. However, service businesses, like law firms, have lots of income, and relatively few deductions. They might prefer the cash method. Heavy industries, like steel mills, have income all right, but they also have huge deductions, for salaries, raw materials, etc. They might prefer the accrual method.

Of course, we do not always get the goods today and pay tomorrow. Sometimes, we prepay. Consider, for example, a magazine subscription. You pay now, and the publisher delivers a year's worth of magazines later. That situation is dealt with specifically in § 455. Other unique prepayment situations are dealt with specifically in the statute and the regulations.

B. The Annual Accounting System

Let's say you contract to build a bridge. It will take five years to build it. Really, you won't know if you made money or lost money, until the bridge is finished five years from now. You would prefer to wait until the bridge is built to report the transaction on your tax return. Only then will you know if you have income or loss.

Basically, you can't do that. The government is spending money every year, so they need you to report your income or loss, and, of course, pay tax, every year. They can't wait five years for you to figure things out. This concept is called the Annual Accounting System. It necessarily follows from this concept that sometimes you will report income or deductions that, as it turns out later, you shouldn't have reported. So, what happens if you're wrong?

C. Mistakes

What if you report taxable income in Year 1, but it turns out in Year 2 that it wasn't taxable income, and you give it back? Conversely, what if you take a deduction in Year 1, but for some reason your transferee gives the money back in Year 2? First of all, if you make a common mistake on your tax return—say, an arithmetic mistake or simply forgetting something—you have three years to correct it with an amended return. But some cases of mistaken income and mistaken deductions are special.

1. *Mistaken Income*

Section 1341 has three elements:

(1)   You reported an item of income in a prior year (let's say in Year 1) because it appeared that you had an unrestricted right to it;

(2)   The item is $3,000 or more; and

(3)   It was established after the close of that prior year (let's say that it was established in Year 3) that you did not have an unrestricted right to such item.

Let's say that your boss gave you a $5,000 bonus in Year 1, because you were the top salesman. You duly report the bonus as taxable income. In Year 3, your boss tells you that he was wrong. You were not the top salesman in Year 1. Your boss demands that you return the money, and you comply. That scenario satisfies the three requirements of § 1341. You reported the $5,000 in Year 1, the item was in excess of $3,000, and, in Year 3, it was established that you had to give it back.

Now, what happens? You deduct the $5,000. But do you deduct it in Year 1 or Year 3? Section 1341 says that you deduct it in the year that it does you, the taxpayer, the most good. How great is that?

2. *Mistaken Deductions*

Mistaken deductions are a bit different. If you take a deduction in Year 1, and you learn in Year 3 that you should not have taken the deduction, then you take that item back into income in Year 3. That's it. There is no going back to Year 1 to see whether that would have been better or worse. There is no reason why mistaken income and mistaken deductions work out so differently; they just do.

There is, however, one more thing about mistaken deductions. That is the **Tax Benefit Rule**. You only take the mistaken deduction back into income in the later year (Year 3) if that deduction actually reduced your income in Year 1. If the mistaken deduction gave you no "tax benefit," then you don't have to put it back into income in the later year.

CHAPTER X

Capital Gains and Losses

I bought Apple Stock in January, 2010 for $10,000. In December of 2014, I sold it for $15,000. I have gain of $5,000.

Amount realized	$15,000
- Basis	$10,000
Gain	$5,000

Simple enough. Why should that $5,000 of gain be taxed any differently from $5,000 of salary or rent? I, for one, think it shouldn't. However, it certainly is different in a number of respects.

First, that $5,000 of salary or rent was all earned and paid this year. In contrast, the gain on the sale of stock accrued over a five-year period. For a while, we had our doubts about income that didn't all happen within the same taxable year.

Other objections flow from that one. First, let's say that the fair market value of my stock actually increased ratably over the entire period. Here are the stock values at the end of each year:

December 2010	$11,000
December 2011	$12,000
December 2012	$13,000
December 2013	$14,000
December 2014	$15,000

Why didn't I pay tax on the $1,000 at the end of each year? Because there was no realization event until December of 2014. Earlier, we talked about the good side of realization—that you can defer the taxable event until you sell. Here's the bad side of realization. When you do sell, then all those years of taxable appreciation get bunched up into the one year. Consider—if you had paid tax on the $1,000 unrealized appreciation in each of those five years, maybe all of that income would have been taxed at the same, low bracket. However, if you bunch all of it into one year, maybe that bunched income will kick you up into a higher bracket in 2014. Bummer.

Second, when I receive that salary or rent all in one year, inflation isn't really a factor. However, when I buy the stock in 2010 and sell it in 2014, it's quite possible that some or all of that gain is merely due to inflation. It's not that the value of my stock went up. Rather, it's that the value of a dollar went down. In fact, the purchasing power of the $10,000 I started with is pretty much the same as the purchasing power of the $15,000 I ended up with. And yet I still pay tax on the gain. Bummer.

Note that both bunching and inflation get worse, the longer I hold on to the stock. There is a lot more bunching over 50 years than over 5 years. Similarly, inflation is a much more likely culprit, the longer I held on to the asset in question. So, we give special treatment to long term capital gains. But long term gains happen when you sell something that you've held for more than a year. How much more bunching and inflation happen when you hold the asset for 13 months, rather than 11 months?

There is a third reason to tax capital gains differently. Arguably, we want taxpayers to acquire capital assets. If we tax gains on those assets at lower rates, then taxpayers will be more likely to acquire capital assets in the first place.

None of these arguments make a whole lot of sense, at least here in the United States. Again, bunching is simply the flip side of realization. If you want to enjoy the tax deferral possibilities of the realization requirement, then you have to put up with the bunching problem on the back end. If you really don't like it, eliminate the realization requirement. Or do income averaging, or use a system of bands, as they do in the United Kingdom. For example, in the UK, assets held for up to a year might be in the first band, with no reduction in the tax rate. Assets held from one to five years might be in the second band, with a small reduction. Assets held from five to fifteen years might be in the third band, with a larger reduction, and so on.

If inflation is the problem, then don't tax inflation. If I bought the stock for $10,000 in 2010, and there was 50% inflation between 2010 and 2014, then index the basis up to $15,000. Then, when you sell, the computation will look like this:

Amount realized	$15,000
- Indexed basis	$15,000
Gain	$0

Alternatively, since inflation is much more likely the longer you hold the asset, use the British system.

The notion of lowering taxes on capital gains to stimulate purchases of capital assets is also problematic. All activity is deterred if it is taxed. If you tax my salary, I may not work so hard.

So maybe wages should be taxfree. If you tax my gains on capital assets, I may buy fewer capital assets. So maybe capital gains should be taxfree. Why is buying capital assets to be preferred over labor? Anyway, if, as you will see, it's not entirely clear, even to tax lawyers, what a capital asset is, then how do the taxpayers know what it is that you are stimulating?

Maybe there is such stimulation of investment. Leave that one to the economists. But here's one that makes little sense. Some have argued that stimulating investment in capital assets will improve the economy so much that we will gain more in tax revenue from the increased salaries of the new employees, etc., than we will lose by not taxing capital gains so much. That's a pretty steep hill to climb.

A. Mechanics

Long term capital gains and losses occur when you have gains or losses from the sale or exchange of a capital asset which you held for more than a year. Short term capital gains and losses occur when you have gains or losses from the sale or exchange of a capital asset which you held for not more than a year.

First, separate all of your sales and exchanges of capital assets into long term transactions and short term transactions. Then, net out the long term transactions, resulting in either a net long term capital gain or a net long term capital loss. Then, net out the short term transactions, resulting in either a net short term capital gain, or a net short term capital loss. If your net long term capital gains exceed your net short term capital losses, then you have a "net capital gain," which receives favorable treatment under § 1(h).

If you don't have any net short term capital losses, either because your short term transactions net out to net short term capital gains, or because you have no short term transactions at all, then your net short term capital losses are zero. Subtract that zero from your net long term capital gains, and, once again, you have a net capital gain, subject to favorable tax treatment.

On the loss side, remember, not all losses are deductible. Generally speaking, business losses are deductible; personal losses are not. So, if a loss is personal, and therefore nondeductible, it doesn't matter if it was capital or ordinary. It's still nondeductible.

Assume that your capital losses are deductible. As you saw above, they must first be used to offset capital gains, no matter whether long term or short term. If the capital losses, long or short, exceed the capital gains (long or short), then the excess losses are only deductible to the extent of $3,000 per year ($1,500 if married filing separately). The rest is carried over into future years.

B.   What Is a Capital Asset?

§ 1221.   Capital asset defined.

(a)   In general—For purposes of this subtitle, the term "capital asset" means property held by the taxpayer (whether or not connected with trade or business), but does not include—

(1)   Stock in trade of the taxpayer or other property of a kind which would properly be included in the inventory of the taxpayer if on hand at the close of the taxable year, or property held by the taxpayer primarily for sale to customers in the ordinary course of his trade or business.

. . .

That's enough of the statute for now. "Capital gains" are property held by the taxpayer. That's pretty much everything. But it does not include inventory. For example, when the grocery store sells you a bunch of broccoli, the grocery store is not taxed on the favorable capital gains rates. Instead, it is taxed at ordinary income rates. That broccoli is part of the grocery store's inventory.

Why? Because a capital gain is supposed to be an extraordinary event—an investment event. If all retail sales were taxed at capital gains rates, then most gains would be capital. We can't afford that.

Similarly, consider ". . .property held by the taxpayer primarily for sale to customers in the ordinary course of his trade or business." That looks a whole lot like inventory. If you sell a house at a gain, and you held that house primarily for sale to customers in the ordinary course of your business, then that sale was *not* an extraordinary event. It's what you do, and it should be taxed at ordinary rates. But, if you lived in the house for 10 years, and then sold it, and didn't sell another house for another 15 years, then those sales *are* extraordinary events.

How do you tell which property is held primarily for sale to customers in the ordinary course of your trade or business? The word "primarily" helps. That means "of first importance." From there on, though, it gets tricky.

Basically, it's a facts and circumstances test. The two most important factors are *frequency of sales* and *substantiality of sales*. Other factors mostly address how much time and effort you put into selling. But, it's a bit more nuanced than that. It's quite possible that, when you sell your first widget in Year 1, it's a capital asset, but that, as you continue to sell more and more widgets over time, eventually, you turn into a seller of widgets, and the subsequent gains become ordinary. Good luck with that.

Let's look briefly at some other statutory exceptions. According to § 1221(a)(3), everything in the world is a capital asset *except*:

A copyright, literary, musical or artistic composition, a letter or memorandum, or similar property, held by—

(A)   A taxpayer whose personal efforts created such property.

Imagine that Jane spends an entire year producing an oil painting. Her expenses on canvas, brushes and paint are negligible, and she ends up selling the painting for $100,000. What did she do to increase the market value of the canvas and paint from essentially zero to $100,000? She put her talent and effort into the painting. In effect, the $100,000 is compensation for her year of labor. Labor income is the epitome of ordinary income. It should not be taxed at favorable, capital gains rates. So Jane pays tax at ordinary income rates.

However, when Jane sells the painting to Becky for $100,000, and Becky resells it five years later for $175,000, Becky's $75,000 gain might well be taxed at capital gains rates. Pursuant to the statute, Becky was not the ". . .taxpayer whose personal efforts created such property." In fact, in Becky's hands, the painting looks much more like an investment—just the sort of thing that the capital gains rates were intended to promote.

Now, consider a composer of country and western songs. She sells her entire catalog of songs at once. Ordinary income pursuant to § 1221(a)(3)? No. Have a look at § 1221(b)(3):

Sale or exchange of self-created musical works.—At the election of the taxpayer, paragraphs (1) and (3) of subsection (a) shall not apply to musical compositions or copyrights in musical works sold or exchanged by a taxpayer described in subsection (a)(3).

Why do composers get this special election? Why do composers get a tax benefit that painters and novelists do not? Because painters and novelists, relatively speaking, are scattered around the country. Country music composers are pretty much concentrated in Nashville. That means that they were able to bring a lot of political pressure on the Tennessee congressional delegation. In fact, they staged "guitar pulls," in which country music composers would bring their guitars to the offices of their Congresspersons. Then, they would pass the guitars around, and sing their songs. In one such event, Senator Lamar Alexander of Tennessee not only attended the guitar pull; he joined in, giving a pretty good rendition of "My Tears Stained My Beer."

C. Other Capital Gains Case Law

In Corn Products Refining Co. v. Commissioner, 350 U.S. 46 (1955), the taxpayer bought corn on the futures market. In other words, it purchased options to buy corn, yet to be harvested, at a set price. Its goal was to protect itself against a rise in prices. If it turned out that it did not need to exercise the option, then it could sell the option. For example, assume that it purchased the option to buy corn, when harvested, at $5 per bushel. If the market price at harvest time of a bushel of corn turned out to be $8 per bushel, then it could exercise the option, and save the $3. However, if it did not need the corn, then it could sell the option to someone else.

The issue was the tax treatment of the sale of the options. The Court held that the options were integrally related to the purchase of inventory. Sale of the inventory would have generated ordinary income, not capital gains. Therefore, sale of the options should have the same result.

The specific case of inventory is now addressed by statute. See §§ 1221(a)(7) and 1221(b)(2). However, more generally, Arkansas Best Corp. v. Commissioner, 485 U.S. 212 (1988) has limited the holding of Corn Products considerably. Corn Products is pretty much limited to its facts.

In Arrowsmith v. Commissioner, 344 U.S. 6 (1952), a corporation was liquidated. Years after the liquidation, its former shareholders had to pay a judgment that related to the old corporation. Had the judgment been paid before the liquidation, it would have been paid out of corporate assets. That would have reduced the amount paid to shareholders upon liquidation. That would, in turn, have reduced the shareholders' capital gain on liquidation. And what is it that reduces capital gains? Why capital losses of course.

The taxpayers argued that, when the judgment was paid in 1944, the corporation did not exist any more. Therefore, the payment had to be deductible as an ordinary expense. Looking back at the tax returns of the corporation for the prior years when the events leading up to the judgment happened would be tantamount to reopening a prior year's return, which would violate the annual accounting system. No, said the Supreme Court. We're not reopening a prior year's return, we're just peeking at it, to determine if the payment should be capital or ordinary. Therefore, having peeked, the payment is treated as a capital loss.

In Hort v. Commissioner, 313 U.S. 28 (1941), tenant made a one-time payment to landlord to get out of a lease. Landlord argued that the payment was the amount realized for the sale of leasehold rights, therefore capital gain. No, said the Supreme Court. The payment was a substitute for the rentals that should have been paid. The rentals would have been ordinary income; so was the lump sum payment.

Hort is kind of scary, in that all sales proceeds reflect the fair market value of the sold asset. And what creates that fair market value? It is the discounted value of the future stream of income. So all sales proceeds should be ordinary. That clearly isn't the case, but how do we draw the line?

Some attempts to draw the line have happened involved lottery winners. In each of these cases, taxpayers won the lottery, and received the right to a stream of payments over time. In each of these cases, taxpayers sold their rights to future income for a one-time payment. Capital gains?

D. Quasi-Capital Assets

In order to expand the application of the lower capital gains rates, Congress did two things. First, it extended the treatment to some assets that are not § 1221 capital assets. Second, it extended the treatment to some transactions that are not sales or exchanges.

Not all assets are capital assets. Section 1221 specifically excludes trade or business depreciable property from the definition of capital asset. So, to expand the benefits of capital gain taxation, Congress created a new category, "property used in the trade or business," in § 1231(b), which includes trade or business depreciable property. However, even "property used in the trade or business" must still not be inventory, or property held by the taxpayer primarily for sale to customers in the ordinary course of his trade or business. Recognized gains and losses from the sales or exchanges of "property used in the trade or business" will be Section 1231 gains and losses.

Moreover, not all gains and losses associated with capital assets are capital gains and losses. According to § 1222, there has to be a "sale or exchange." Thefts are not sales or exchanges, nor are government condemnations of property. Congress, in § 1231, changed that as well. Section 1231 also extends Section 1231 gain and loss treatment to compulsory or involuntary conversions, even though there was no sale or exchange.

What happens to Section 1231 gains and losses? You net them out. If they net out as positive, then all of them are treated as long-term capital transactions. Therefore, they are then thrown in with the "real," § 1221 long term gains and losses, and treated accordingly. If they net out as negative, then they are all treated as ordinary gains and losses. Pretty much heads taxpayer wins, tails government loses.

CHAPTER XI

Who Is the Taxpayer?

You would think that we always know who the taxpayer is. The IRS knows that my salary is taxable to me, because my name is written on the check, and my employer has to tell the IRS that they paid me. But sometimes, it's not so easy.

A. What Is at Stake

Consider single taxpayers John and Joe. This year, John has taxable income of $0, Joe has taxable income of $500,000. Let's say that a dollar of additional taxable income comes flying down the street. Does it matter if it's taxable to John or Joe? Of course it does.

Say that dollar is taxable to John. Then, it will be added to John's taxable income of $0. John's total taxable income will therefore be $1, taxable at the lowest possible rate, or not at all.

Say that dollar is taxable to Joe. Then, it will be added to Joe's taxable income of $500,000. Joe's total taxable income will therefore be $500,001. That dollar will be taxable at the highest possible rate.

But that's only the beginning. Given our progressive rate structure, income splitting is a terrific idea. Consider a single taxpayer, A, who has $500,000 of taxable income. His tax will be around $150,000. Now imagine that the same $500,000 is split among five single taxpayers, B, C, D, E, and F, each of whom pays tax on $100,000. The tax on $50,000 is around $18,000. Five times $18,000 is $90,000. Ninety thousand dollars is a whole lot less than $150,000. Why is the tax on B, C, D, E and F so much less? Because only $9,500 of A's income is taxed at the lowest rate of 10%. Three hundred thousand of it is taxed at 35%. In contrast, each of B, C, D, E, and F have their first $9,500 taxed at 10%. Among the five of them, that's $47,500 taxed at 10%. On the other hand, none of the income of B through F is taxed at 35%. In fact, the highest rate any one of them pays is only 24%.

If a high bracket person is taxable, then she will pay tax at high rates. If a low bracket person is taxable, then she will pay tax at low rates. Should the high bracket person transfer her income to the low bracket person? No. If you transfer the income, you don't have it any more. Better to keep the income, even if you do have to pay taxes at higher rates.

Similarly, if the high bracket person splits her income with other, lower bracket individuals, then the aggregate tax will be lowered. Should she do that? No, because then she doesn't have the income any more.

The trick, then, is to get the income taxed to someone else, and/or split the income, without having to give it away. That's not easy to do. However, if you can give the income (or share it) to someone you were going to give it to anyway, now you're talking. Most likely, those people are members of your family. See also Chapter XII.

B. **Assignment of Income**

This is a caselaw doctrine. It works best with gratuitous transfers, such as transfers to family members. Let's say you have income producing property—a fruit tree. You want the fruit to be taxable to your son, not to you. To be successful, you must do two things. First, you must make the transfer before the fruit has ripened (Timing). Second, you must transfer the tree, not just the fruit (Control).

Why timing? Because, if you wait until the fruit is ripe, then it is already taxable to you. Furthermore, you can spend the entire growing season lording it over your son, telling him that, if he doesn't clean up his act, you won't give him the fruit. After you've had all that fun, you should surely pay the tax.

Why control? Imagine that you keep the tree, and tell your son that you are assigning whatever fruit the tree might produce to him. Such an assignment does not prevent you from chopping down the tree. Also, that assignment doesn't require you to water the tree, or to fertilize it. In effect, you are assigning the fruit to your son, but you are retaining control over whether there will be any fruit, and, if so, how much. In that instance, the owner or the tree gets taxed on the fruit. In the words of Justice Holmes, ". . .we think that no distinction can be taken according to the motives leading to the arrangement by which the fruits are attributed to a different tree from that on which they grew." Lucas v. Earl, 281 U.S. 111 (1929). That is the doctrine of fruit and tree. Be careful, however. Like many of Holmes' pithy pronouncements, it can often be misleading.

C. Income Splitting with Other Entities—C Corporations

The assignment of income cases typically involve gratuitous transfers to family members. You can also split your income with a corporation, partnership, or trust. The same tax-saving principles generally apply.

Using a standard corporation (generally referred to as "C Corporations" because they are described in Subchapter C or the Code), however, is not always a good idea. The income of C Corporations can be taxed twice. Recall that dividends are not deductible to the corporation. If a C Corporation earns income, it will be taxed at the corporate level. That's one tax. If the corporation then pays a dividend to its shareholders, the dividend payments will be nondeductible to the corporation, and taxable to the shareholders. That's the second tax. Are you sure you want to do that?

It is the double tax that leads to disguised dividends, described in Chapter V. It also leads to funding corporations (or claiming to) with bonds rather than stock. The interest payments on bonds are deductible; dividend payments on stock is not. It also leads to the formation (or claimed formation) of partnerships rather than corporations. Partnership income flows through the partnership, to be taxed only once, at the partner level. That's a better deal than the double tax on corporate income.

For all of these reasons, many have argued that the United States should adopt the European model of corporate tax integration. Using such a model, corporations and partnerships would be taxed the same. All income would flow through the corporations and partnerships taxfree, to be taxed only once, at the shareholder or partner level.

Corporate tax integration contemplates eliminating the tax at the corporate level, leaving just the one tax at the shareholder level. In the United States, we have gone halfway toward the one-tax idea, but in a rather cockeyed way. We have created a large category of dividends called Qualified Dividends. Such dividends are taxable to the shareholders, but at much lower rates. Therefore, essentially, we have retained the tax at the corporate level, but we have lowered the tax at the shareholder level. In effect, we have replaced two taxes with one and a half taxes.

CHAPTER XII

Families

Families give rise to lots of neat tax schemes, because your family members are precisely those sorts of folks to whom you might actually want to give your money. So, if you can get it taxed to them instead of to you, you might be better off, even if it means giving it to them. But that leads to some more general questions about groups.

Most of us don't live alone. Most of us live in groups. Group living is not just a social thing; it's a financial thing. To one extent or another, those groups pool group income and pool group expenses. How should the tax code take these group living arrangements into account?

Maybe we shouldn't. In fact, if you read the Internal Revenue Code, you'd get the distinct impression that the taxpayer is the individual, not the group. But, as it turns out, we do take group living arrangements into account, sometimes.

A. Marriage

Husbands and wives pool their income, and their expenses, more or less. Usually, they live in one house, or one apartment. So their housing expenses are for the two of them—not just one. Also, they have one refrigerator. When they buy groceries, they buy them as a couple—not individually. So what to do?

Let's start with the income side of things.

1. The Joint Return

Let's say that Husband earns $38,700 this year, and Wife earns exactly the same. Together, they earn $77,400. They can do their taxes using the Married Filing Joint Returns schedules, or they can use the Married Filing Separate Returns schedules. Using the Tax Tables, if they file a joint return, their tax bill will be $8,913. If they file separate returns, then Husband will owe $4,459, and Wife will owe $4,459. Two times $4,459 is $8,918. That's really, really close to the $8,913 they would have paid if they filed a joint return. It turns out that the couple pays essentially the same tax, whether they file Married Filing Separate, or a Joint Return.

I know this because I looked at Sections 1(j)(2)(A) and (D), which have the tax rates from now until 2025. I also looked at the Tax Tables that go with the Form 1040 Instructions. If you like, you can check for yourselves. Better yet, you can just trust me.

The "Married Filing Separate" rates came first. To determine the "Married Filing Joint Returns" tax, take the spouses' aggregate income and divide it by two. Apply the Married Filing Separate rates to that result. Then, multiply the tax result by two, and you have the "Married Filing Joint Returns" tax. In effect, the "Married Filing Joint Returns" rates conclusively presume that exactly 50% of the taxable income is earned by Husband, and the other 50% is earned by Wife.

The Joint Return, created by Congress in 1948, was a tax break for married couples. Any tax break for marrieds must necessarily be a tax penalty for singles. In fact, after 1948, in some cases, singles paid 40% more tax than a married couple with the same aggregate income. To ameliorate this penalty, the single taxpayer rates, which are lower than the married filing separately rates, were created in 1969.

2. *Marriage Penalties and Bonuses*

Now, single taxpayers have the advantage of the singles rates, and the disadvantage of the lack of access to the income-splitting of the joint return. Married couples whose income is already pretty evenly split don't need the joint return, and suffer from the higher rates. Therefore, they suffer the **marriage penalty.** Married couples whose income is not evenly split get an income-splitting advantage from the joint return that outweighs the penalty of the higher rates. Those couples get a **marriage bonus.**

Can the tax rates be structured so that neither marriage penalties nor singles penalties exist? Not as long as we have progressive rates. Imagine a tax system in which income up to $10,000 is taxed at 10%, while income in excess of $10,000 is taxed at 20%.

Assume the following taxpayers, income, and tax:

Taxpayer	Income	Tax
Alex	$10,000	$1,000
Becky	$10,000	$1,000
Charles	$0	$0
Deborah	$20,000	$3,000
Eddie	$20,000	$3,000

Deborah and Eddie owe $3,000 in taxes. For each of them, the first $10,000 of income is taxed at 10%. That's $1,000 in tax. The remaining income of $10,000 is taxed at 20%. That's $2,000 in tax. Add the two together, and you get $3,000 in tax.

Now imagine that Alex marries Becky, and Charles marries Deborah. Eddie remains single.

Taxpayer	Income	Tax	A. Aggregate Tax with No Change	B. Joint Return	C. Tax on Family Income of $20,000
Alex	$10,000	$1,000	$2,000	$2,000	$3,000
Becky	$10,000	$1,000			
Charles	$0	$0	$3,000	$2,000	$3,000
Deborah	$20,000	$3,000			
Eddie	$20,000	$3,000	$3,000	N/A	$3,000

If we just aggregate the tax with no change [Column A], Charles and Deborah will be upset. Why are they paying $3,000 on their combined $20,000 of income, while Alex and Becky are paying only $2,000 on their combined $20,000 of income?

On the other hand, if we let Alex & Becky and Charles & Deborah file joint returns [Column B], then Eddie will be upset. Why should he pay $3,000 on his $20,000 of income, while the two married couples pay only $2,000 on their identical $20,000 in income?

Finally, if we just tax each household on its $20,000 in household income, using the original rates [Column C], then Alex and Becky will ask why, when they were single, they each paid only $1,000 tax on their $10,000 of income, while, after the marriage, they are paying a $1,500 share of tax on the same income.

In fact, there are three goals which an income tax system might have:

1) Progressive rates

2) Marriage neutrality—treating married couples with the same aggregate income the same; and

3) Fairness as between marrieds and singles.

It is impossible for one tax system to accomplish more than two of the three goals. Has our system made the right choices? Is marriage neutrality even a laudable goal? Perhaps we should tax Charles and Deborah at higher rates to mitigate the unfairness of not taxing the imputed income from the household services which Charles is providing. For that matter, who deserves a tax break— marrieds or singles? Should singles get the break because they don't enjoy the same economies of scale in living expenses that marrieds do?

When the income of a married couple is split 100%-0%, the tax advantages of marriage are at their highest. That's because the benefits of the joint return's income-splitting outweigh the higher married rates. Conversely, when the income is split 50-50, the tax disadvantages of being married are at their highest. That's because the income is already split, so that the joint return doesn't help at all. The break-even point is around 80%-20%. If the spouse earning the lesser income earns less than 20% of the total, then there is a marriage bonus. If the spouse earning the lesser income earns more than 20% of the total, then there is a marriage penalty.

Note that only higher income couples can afford for one of the two spouses not to earn income outside the home. Therefore, higher income couples tend to get a marriage bonus. Lower income couples tend to get a marriage penalty.

3. *Same Sex Marriage*

After the Supreme Court invalidated part of the Defense of Marriage Act in United States v. Windsor, 133 S.Ct. 2675 (2013), the IRS responded with Revenue Ruling 2013-17. Now, same-sex couples who are lawfully married will be married for the purposes of the Internal Revenue Code, including the requirement that they compute their taxes either under the joint return schedules or the married filing separately schedules. Those who enter into registered domestic partnerships or civil unions, however, will not be treated as married. According to the Ruling, a couple is lawfully married if the marriage was lawful in the state in which they were married.

Note that, under this new legal landscape, the definition of marriage has changed, but the tax consequences have not. Therefore, a same-sex married couple in which one partner earns 100% of the household income and the other 0% would be better off married, for tax purposes, while a same-sex married couple in which each partner earns 50% of the household income would be better off single, for tax purposes.

B. Divorce

1. *Alimony*

Divorce is, of course, a highly significant personal and emotional event; it is also a highly significant financial event. First, there are often substantial payments and transfers of property from one ex-spouse to the other. Second, all of the efficiencies and economies of scale disappear, as the couple transitions from maintaining one household to maintaining two. Finally, there are often substantial legal fees involved.

For all of these reasons, divorce has had important tax consequences to the parties, for most of our income tax history.

Those tax consequences flowed crucially from the characterization of transfers as either **alimony** or **property settlements**. **Alimony** was usually preferable, because alimony payments were deductible to the payor spouse, and taxable to the payee spouse. **Property settlements**, on the other hand, were neither deductible to the payor spouse, nor were they taxable to the payee spouse. Since the payor spouse was usually in a higher tax bracket, **alimony** characterization usually meant that the payments would be taxable at a lower rate. In effect, it was a form of income-splitting—perhaps to recognize the financial hardship of divorce.

However, the Tax Cuts and Jobs Act has repealed the alimony deduction and inclusion provisions. For divorces entered into after January 1, 2019, payments from one spouse to the other will not be deductible by the payor spouse, and they will not be includible in the income of the payee spouse.

2. Transfers of Appreciated (or Depreciated) Property

Section 1041 provides that, when a spouse transfers property to a former spouse, and the transfer is incident to the divorce, no gain or loss shall be recognized, and the transferee picks up the transferor's basis. Imagine that Wife owned Greenacre with a basis of $15,000. When it was worth $100,000, she transferred it to Husband, incident to their divorce. First, Wife recognizes no gain on the transfer. Second, Husband picks up Wife's basis of $15,000. If Husband were to sell Greenacre the next day, presumably for $100,000, then he, not she, would be taxable on the $85,000. And you thought the divorce itself was punishment enough.

Section 1041 speaks in terms of transfers. Therefore, it is irrelevant if the transfer looked like a sale, or a gift. It is also irrelevant whether Husband transferee gave no consideration for Greenacre, or even full consideration. The tax results are the same.

Section 1041 works whether the property went up in value, or down. Also, § 1041 applies not only to transfers incident to divorce, but also to all transfers of property between a husband and wife, during the marriage. The planning possibilities are quite intriguing.

C. Children

How large a family should you have? Each woman should have 2.1 children, if we want to keep the population of the country stable. Is that what we want? Would we rather let the domestic birth rate go down, and make up the difference with immigration? In any event, to what extent should our tax laws impact these choices? Admittedly, it is hard to imagine that someone would decide to have a child or not based solely on tax laws. However, tax laws can do two things. First, they might push some folks one way or the other, at the margin. Second, they are in effect a statement by the legislature about what we think is important. So, are children important?

Different countries do different things. Some countries limit the tax breaks to a stated number of children. In others, the number of tax breaks is unlimited. In some, the tax break goes up for the second and subsequent child. In others, it goes down. Perhaps there are economies of scale, or the older kids can baby sit for the younger ones. I have always felt that the tax break for children should be a function of the weight of the child, but, so far, no one has taken me up on that. Needless to say, to analyze the policy of another country toward children, one should not merely look at their tax laws, but at all of their governmental policies. Yet, even just looking at their tax laws, one should be sure to look at all of them. In the United States, for example, we have the child tax credit, the adoption tax credit, and the household and dependent care credit, among others. Previously, we had the personal and dependency exemptions See below. One should also look at subsidies for education and child care, and a host of other things.

1. Personal and Dependency Exemptions

For most of our history, the tax laws provided a pretty generous personal exemption for the taxpayer, and equally generous dependency exemptions for his or her dependents, no matter how many. There were, however, some complications as to what a "dependent" was. Now, these personal and dependency exemptions have been eliminated. Instead, the standard deduction has been increased. We lose the individual fairness of adjusting the tax bill for family size, but we do gain an increase in simplicity.

2. The Child Tax Credit and the Adoption Expenses Credit

Section 23 provides the Adoption Expenses credit. It is capped at $10,000, but it phases down for adjusted gross incomes in excess of $150,000.

Section 24 provides the Child tax credit. It is capped at $2,000 per qualifying child, but it phases down for adjusted gross incomes in excess of $400,000 for a joint return, $200,000 for an unmarried individual.

3. The Kiddie Tax

Say you have an interest-bearing account. You are in the 35% tax bracket, and your infant son is in the 15% tax bracket. You transfer the account to your son, in the hope that he will be taxed at the lower rate. Fat chance. Pursuant to § 1(g), the income will be taxable at the marginal rate for trust income, until the child reaches his 18th birthday.

In some ways, Section 73 is the reverse of § 1(g). According to § 73, a child is taxable upon that child's income earned from the services of the child, even if the money is actually paid to the parent. Of course, the kicker is to prove that the money was earned by the child, for the child's services.

4. *Child Care Tax Credit*

See coverage of this credit *infra*, in Chapter VIII.

Installment Sales

You bought a widget for $10,000. Now you sell it for $50,000. If you sold it for one payment, the calculation would be easy:

Amount realized	$50,000
– Basis	$10,000
Gain	$40,000

However, what if you sold it for five annual payments of $10,000?

You could tax the Year 1 payment:

Amount realized	$10,000
– Basis	$10,000
Gain	$0

Now that you've used up your basis, the payments received in Years 2 through 5 could all be:

Amount realized	$10,000
– Basis	$0
Gain	$10,000

Your gain over the five years would be:

Year 1	0
Year 2	$10,000
Year 3	$10,000
Year 4	$10,000
Year 5	$10,000

Your gain over the five year period would be the same $40,000 that you would have recognized if you had sold the widget for the lump sum payment of $50,000, but something doesn't seem quite right.

Instead, consult § 453. Under § 453(b), an "installment sale" means:

> A disposition of property where at least 1 payment is to be received after the close of the taxable year in which the disposition occurs.

So far, so good. The widget was sold in Year 1, but payments were received in Years 1, 2, 3, 4 and 5.

If you have an installment sale, how is the gain computed? That's set out in § 453(c), which defines "installment method" as:

> A method under which the income recognized for any taxable year from a disposition is that proportion of the payments received in that year which the *gross profit* (realized or to be realized when payment is completed) bears to the *total contract price*.

In this case, the total contract price is $50,000. The gross profit is:

Amount realized	$50,000
- Basis	$10,000
Gross profit	$40,000

The ratio of gross profit to total contract price is:

$$\frac{\text{Gross profit}}{\text{Total contract price}} = \frac{\$40,000}{\$50,000} = 80\%$$

So, 80% of each $10,000 payment will be recognized gain. Therefore, for each of the $10,000 payments, 80%, or $8,000, will be recognized as gain. Over the five years, five times $8,000, or $40,000, will be recognized gain. It's the same number, but now it is spread out over the term of the installment contract.

Nonrecognition Transactions

A. Like Kind Exchanges

Let's say you buy real estate (Blackacre) that has the potential to be developed as a golf course, for $100,000 in Year 1. In Year 5, when Blackacre is worth $300,000, you trade it for Whiteacre, which is also real estate which has the potential to be developed as a golf course.

One would think that you would be taxed on $200,000 of gain. Your amount realized is the cash of zero plus the fair market value of the property received—$300,000.

Amount realized	$300,000
– Basis	$100,00
Gain	$200,000

Let's take a moment, however, to consider why we wait for the realization event. The realization event provides us with easy valuation. Also, the sale provides the taxpayer with the liquid assets with which to pay the tax.

Neither valuation nor liquidity is easy in this exchange. Valuation is only accomplished if you know the appraised value of Whiteacre. Liquidity isn't there at all, because, when the transaction is completed, you have no cash. All you have is Whiteacre, which is every bit as illiquid as Blackacre was.

Further, in a very real sense, you have not disinvested. To be sure, you no longer own Blackacre. However, you still have your original investment tied up in real estate with the potential for development as a golf course. This exchange of Whiteacre for Blackacre is not an opportune time to tax. It would be better to wait until a final cashing out.

That is essentially what § 1031 does. Section 1031(a)(1) provides:

> No gain or loss shall be recognized on the exchange of property held for productive use in a trade or business or for investment if such property is exchanged solely for property of like kind which is held either for productive use in a trade or business or for investment.

Blackacre was held for productive use or investment, and it was exchanged solely for Whiteacre. Whiteacre, being held for the same reason as Blackacre, is property of like kind. Therefore, according to § 1031, there will be no gain or loss.

Section 1031(d) provides that your basis in Blackacre of $100,000 will carry over to be your basis in Whiteacre. Thus, if you turn around and sell Whiteacre for cash of $300,000, you will then have gain of $200,000:

Amount realized	$300,000
– Basis	$100,000
Gain	$200,000

However, you probably won't sell Whiteacre the next day. You'll surely hold on to it for a while. So, what Section 1031 accomplishes is deferral of the gain, as if no realization event had occurred.

That's what happens if you exchange Blackacre solely for Whiteacre. But what happens if you exchange Blackacre for Whiteacre plus something else? That something else could be cash, or property. Either way, we call it *"boot."*

Let's say that you exchange Blackacre for Greenacre (fair market value of $250,000) plus cash of $50,000. Section 1031(b), fetchingly titled "Gain from exchanges not solely in kind," provides that the gain will now be recognized, but only up to the boot received.

Thus, the gain of $200,000 will be recognized, but only to the extent of the $50,000 cash received. However, basis might change. Section 1031(d) provides that your new basis in Greenacre will be your old basis in Blackacre-$100,000, but decreased by the amount of cash received, but increased by the amount of gain recognized. Your old basis in Blackacre was $100,000. Your new basis in Whiteacre will be that $100,000, decreased by the $50,000 cash received, but increased by the $50,000 gain recognized. That gets us back to $100,000.

Let's say that you turn around the next day and sell Whiteacre for its fair market value of $250,000: You will recognize gain of another $150,000:

Amount realized	$250,000
- Basis	$100,000
Gain	$150,000

So the $50,000 gain on the exchange of Blackacre for Whiteacre, plus the $150,000 gain on the sale of Whiteacre for cash, equals the full $200,000 of gain that should be recognized, eventually.

Until the passage of the Tax Cuts and Jobs Act in 1917, Section 1031 applied to both real and personal property. However, now, it only applies to real property.

B. Involuntary Conversions

Say you bought a business building for $100,000. When it was worth $300,000, it was totally destroyed in a fire. The insurance company paid out the $300,000, and you used it to replace the building.

General tax principles would say that you should have gain of $200,000:

Amount realized	$300,000
- Basis	$100,000
Gain	$200,000

However, just as was the case with like kind exchanges, you don't have any cash with which to pay a tax. Further, your money is still invested in the business building, more or less as it was before. Again, this isn't a great time to tax.

Accordingly, Section 1033 says that no gain will be recognized, and the basis will be carried over, as long as the new property is "similar or related in service or use" to the old property. But what if you don't reinvest all of the insurance proceeds in the replacement building? Once again, the gain will be recognized, but only to the extent of the boot (the cash that you don't reinvest), and the basis in the converted property will be adjusted. This time, however, you can defer all of the gain even if you initially receive a cash settlement from the insurance company, provided that you take that cash, and use it to acquire replacement property, within the time specified in the statute.

C. Exclusion of Gain from Sale of Principal Residence

Say you bought your personal home in Year 1 for $100,000. In Year 5, when your home was worth $300,000, you sold it for cash, and moved into a retirement facility. Section 121 provides:

> Gross income shall not include gain from the sale or exchange of property if, during the 5 year period ending on the date of the sale or exchange, such property has been owned and used by the taxpayer as the taxpayer's principal residence for periods aggregating 2 years or more.

Section (b)(1) goes on to provide that the amount excluded cannot exceed $250,000, or $500,000 if the taxpayers file a joint return. Here, your gain of $200,000 is below both the $250,000 and the $500,000 caps, so you don't have to pay tax on any of it. Did I tell you that homeownership is great? Of course, you can only get one such exclusion every 2 years, pursuant to § 121(b)(3).

Why do we do this? We want to encourage homeownership. Also, it is quite likely that the homeowners had stayed in that principal residence for a long time. If there is one thing that Americans don't do very well in their personal lives, it's keeping records. What if the homeowners in question have no idea what they paid for their house, say some 20 years before? Section 121 solves that problem, by saying that, for most of us, they won't tax it at all.

CHAPTER XV

Tax Shelters

The classic tax shelter involves using someone else's money to invest in an enterprise that will generate lots of juicy deductions and losses on the front end, but then turn around and start generating taxable income later. If you just let things run their course, you will have deferred taxable income for all of those loss years. Even better, when the enterprise turns around and starts making money, you can trade that investment for another money-losing venture, and play the whole game all over again. What you are trying to accomplish is to create deductions in this enterprise which you can use to offset taxable income in your other enterprises. In short, you are trying to "shelter" your other income from taxes during those loss years.

This classic tax shelter has been mostly shut down, by a number of statutory and case law developments. First, remember that, when you use someone else's money, *Crane* and *Tufts* come into play. You may indeed create basis with borrowed money. However, on the other end of the transaction, the discharge of that debt will be recognized as amount realized.

Second, you don't really want to risk your money; you just want to save on your taxes. The **at-risk** rules provide that, if you don't run any risks, you don't get the deductions. See Section 465.

Third, you don't want to be actively involved in this enterprise. Again, all you want to do is to save taxes. You're just trying to shelter your income. But Section 469 says that if you incur losses from **passive**, not active, activities, then your losses will only be allowable against your income from those very same activities. In short, you will not be allowed to use your *passive* activity losses to shelter your *active* income.

Fourth, there is the **Alternative Minimum Tax**, or AMT. Sometimes, Congress realizes that it has done too much of a good thing. It enacts lots of "tax preferences," never considering that one well-advised taxpayer will use not just one of them, but all of them. Egad, Congress never intended that. You might consider AMT as a bit of Congressional finger crossing.

Pursuant to the AMT, you refigure your taxable income, adding back all of the "tax preferences" listed in §§ 56 and 57. Then, you make sure that you paid at least 26% (or 28% for higher incomes) of that recomputed amount. The AMT is designed with thresholds that are intended to limit its application to the richer people. Those thresholds do not always work out as intended.

Fifth, the **economic substance** rules provide that, if a transaction has no economic substance, it will not be recognized. This is a statutory codification of a case-law doctrine. To give a relatively simple example of a complex rule, if it can be shown that you did something that you absolutely would not have done except for the favorable tax consequences, then that activity has no economic substance. You might want to have a look at § 7701(o). Then again, maybe not.

Finally, there are the **professional responsibility** aspects. Tax lawyers are, of course, lawyers. As such, they are subject to the Model Rules of Professional Conduct. Those Rules might come into play if the lawyer counseled the client to be less than truthful with the IRS. In addition, there is Treasury Department Circular 230. These are rules for admission to practice before the IRS. They require tax attorneys to be really sure that they know both the law and the relevant facts before giving an opinion on a proposed tax shelter. Circular 230 is definitely something to think about, when you consider marketing an aggressive tax shelter scheme to clients.

Then there's § 6662, which imposes an accuracy-related penalty on certain taxpayers who understate their tax liability. That penalty can be reduced in certain situations. However, no reduction is possible if there is a tax shelter involved. See § 6662(d)(2)(C).

Come to think of it, you might also want to have a look at § 6694. That section penalizes the tax return preparer, if he or she prepares a return that understates tax liability due to an unreasonable position. Get it? The penalty is on the preparer, not the taxpayer. That preparer could be you.

CHAPTER XVI

Applications

A. Cinderella

1. Facts

Cinderella was forced to live with her wicked stepmother and two wicked stepsisters. Cinderella had to do all the housework, and was dressed in rags, while the wicked stepmother and stepsisters did nothing all day, and dressed in the finest clothes.

The Handsome Prince threw a ball. Cinderella would have liked to go, but she had nothing to wear. Luckily, her Fairy Godmother magically turned her rags into a beautiful ball gown, and her threadbare shoes into glass slippers. What's more, she turned a pumpkin into a beautiful coach, and some mice into handsome horses. She warned Cinderella, however, that everything would turn back into what it had been before, at the stroke of midnight.

Cinderella went to the ball, and the Handsome Prince fell in love with her. Just before midnight, she ran away. However, she dropped one of her glass slippers.

The next day, the Handsome Prince sent his courtiers all over the kingdom with the glass slipper, declaring that he would marry the girl whose foot fit the slipper. Cinderella's foot fit the slipper. They were married, and lived happily ever after.

2. *Tax Consequences*

The wicked stepmother and stepsisters would have had no taxable income from the value of Cinderella's services. Those services were imputed income within the family unit, which we do not tax.

Assume that Cinderella owned the pumpkin and the mice. Presumably, the fair market value of the coach and horses far exceeded the fair market value of the pumpkin and the mice. However, the pumpkin and the mice were not *exchanged* for the coach and horses; they were *converted* into the coach and horses. Therefore, there was no realization event. Without a realization event, that increase in value was merely unrealized appreciation. Besides, it only lasted a few hours.

Moreover, even if one could argue that the conversion of the pumpkin and the mice were income taxable events, they were accomplished by the actions of the Fairy Godmother, who clearly did them out of detached and disinterested generosity. Therefore, any income would have been excluded as a taxfree gift to Cinderella under § 102.

Presumably, the Handsome Prince's courtiers were away from home overnight while searching for the girl who would fit the glass slipper. Accordingly, they would want to deduct their travel expenses. However, these expenses are employee business expenses. Therefore, they are nondeductible, at least until 2025.

It is assumed that Cinderella had little or no taxable income before she married the Prince. He probably had substantial income.

Therefore, once married, they should have found the joint return to be quite advantageous.

B. Jack and the Beanstalk

1. *Facts*

Jack's parents told him to take the family dairy cow to town and sell it for cash, in order to meet family expenses. Instead, Jack sold the cow for some magic beans. In anger, Jack's parents threw the beans out the window.

The next day, the beans had sprouted into a giant beanstalk. Jack climbed the beanstalk, and found himself in the home of a giant. Jack stole the giant's valuables, including a goose who laid golden eggs. When the giant ran after him, Jack ran down the beanstalk and then chopped it down, killing the giant. Jack and his parents lived happily ever after.

2. *Tax Consequences*

When Jack sold the cow, he was acting as agent for his parents. Even though he did not follow their instructions precisely, he was still their agent, and it was still their cow. Therefore, any gain on the sale of the cow was taxable to the parents, not Jack.

The IRS will argue that Jack's transaction with the seller of the magic beans was an arm's length transaction. Therefore, the fair market value of the cow must have been equal to the fair market value of the beans. Jack's parents' amount realized on the sale of the cow, therefore, should have been the fair market value of the magic beans. Considering subsequent events, that value would have been considerable. The dairy cow, however, would have been "property used in the trade or business" under § 1231(b)(3)(A).

Therefore, at least there would be the possibility of favorable capital gains rates.

Jack's parents will argue that Jack was a bit soft in the head, and therefore incapable of making an arm's length transaction. Accordingly, the amount realized on the sale of the cow for the beans should be negligible. When the beans became the beanstalk, that increase in value should have been unrealized appreciation. Jack's parents' arguments will probably fail.

Jack's theft of the giant's valuables was probably illegal. However, illegal income is still taxable.

If Jack were to sell the goose, it would not be section 1231 property. Section 1231(b)(3), in defining "property used in the trade or business," concludes with the words, "Such term does not include poultry."

C. The Two Little Pigs*

1. Facts

The First Little Pig built a structure out of brick, and the Second Little Pig built a structure out of straw. The Big Bad Wolf was unable to blow the First Little Pig's brick building down. However, he had better luck with the Second Little Pig's straw building. He blew that one down, and ate up the Second Little Pig.

It is assumed that both structures were legitimate business assets. The First Little Pig spent $50,000 to build the brick structure. Due to the excellence of the construction, he incurred no maintenance and repair expenses over the life of the asset.

The Second Little Pig spent $10,000 on the straw structure. Due to its shoddy construction, the Second Little Pig had to incur

---

* For my purposes, the Third Little Pig is irrelevant. Moreover, adding another pig would only make this Short and Happy book longer, and sadder.

considerable expenses for maintenance and repair. In fact, had the Big Bad Wolf not blown it down, the Second Little Pig would have spent $40,000 on maintenance and repair over the estimated useful life of the building.

2. Tax Consequences

Over the useful life of the building, the First Little Pig will be able to deduct $50,000 in depreciation. Had the Second Little Pig's straw building survived for its entire useful life, the Second Little Pig would have deducted $10,000 in depreciation (limited to the $10,000 basis), plus $40,000 in maintenance and repairs. Thus, at the end of the day, both would have been able to take an identical aggregate $50,000 in deductions. The timing of the deductions, however, would differ.

When the Big Bad Wolf blows down the straw building, the Second Little Pig's realized a deductible business loss. It is fortunate that the loss was not a personal casualty loss, because those losses are only deductible if they are attributable to a Presidentially declared disaster, which clearly was not true in this case. Of course, none of this does the Second Little Pig any good, since he will be dead.

D. The Snow Queen

1. Facts

The Snow Queen has an annoying tendency to freeze everything, and everybody, in her vicinity, especially if she waves her hands around in a reckless manner. She ends up freezing her sister half to death, and putting her kingdom into a state of perpetual winter. The Snow Queen retreats to the Ice Palace, where she can live in isolation, and prevent further harm. Her sister, with the help of the Woodcutter and the Snowman, go to the Ice Palace to bring the Snow Queen back. The Snow Queen comes back. Due to an Act of True Love, the Sister, the Snow Queen, and the kingdom are saved. By the way, the Snowman really, really likes summer.

2. *Tax Consequences*

The Snow Queen's tendency to freeze everyone and everything around her is a medical condition. Wearing gloves seems to help. Of course, the gloves do nothing to cure the condition, but they do help her to cope. Crutches and wheelchairs don't cure paralysis, but they are medical expenses even so. So too are the gloves. Assuming that the gloves were specially made, and prescribed by a licensed medical professional, they would count as a medical expense. It is hard, however, to imagine that the cost of a pair of gloves alone would get the Snow Queen anywhere close to the 10% of AGI threshold, especially considering her royal income.

Was the Snow Queen's trip to the Ice Palace a medical trip? The trip was necessitated by her medical condition. However, she didn't do anything at the Ice Palace to cure her condition. So, was the trip "transportation primarily for and essential to medical care"?

Medical expenses include the expenses of curing medical conditions, but also the expenses of coping with medical conditions.

Regulation § 1.213-1(e)(1)(i) provides:

The term "medical care" includes the diagnosis, cure, mitigation, treatment, or prevention of disease.

The word "mitigation" is helpful.

Whose disease? The Snow Queen may not be preventing her own disease, but her isolation surely prevents others from falling ill. Can one incur deductible medical expenses for mitigating the diseases of others? Consider the treatment of tuberculosis in the Nineteenth Century. Tuberculosis victims went to sanitariums to live in isolation, to ensure that others would not catch the disease. Nothing was done to cure them. Wasn't that "medical care"? If these arguments are accepted, then the Snow Queen's trip to the Ice Palace was a medical trip. Of course, given the *Bilder* case, she can deduct the costs of getting there, but not staying there. She can't even get the measly $50 per day provided in § 213(d)(2), since she is not going to a hospital facility.

I raised these issues with the Tax Teachers' Chat Group. The majority believes that the Snow Queen's trip to the Ice Palace would not have been a medical trip. However, I, personally, think that she has a shot. Even if she lost, I don't think that her position would be so unreasonable as to trigger penalties under § 6694. Anyway, if she does lose, she really needs to let it go.

The Snowman wants to spend all of his time in the summer. Clearly, he has a death wish. Despite his apparently happy (sunny?) demeanor, he is, at the very least, clinically depressed. He needs the help of a mental health professional, and the expenses of that help would be medical care.

Presumably, the cost, if any, of the constant snowfall above his head, which allows him to survive in summer climates, is an expense of coping with his mental illness. I could see an argument for a deductible medical expense here, but it would be iffy.

E. Robin Hood

1. Facts

Robin Hood and his Merry Men robbed from the rich and gave to the poor.

2. Tax Consequences

Whatever Robin Hood stole is taxable income to him. The fact that the income is illegally obtained does not make it taxfree.

Robin Hood can get a charitable deduction only if he donates to a qualified charity. Poor people, as such, are not qualified charitable donees. However, if Robin Hood were to give to a qualified charity, such as the Salvation Army, which, in turn, redistributed to poor people, then his donations would be tax deductible.

There is, however, a broader perspective. Robbing from the rich to give to the poor looks a lot like the progressive tax structure. The analogy is even more apt if one believes, along with many libertarians, that taxation is theft. Taxing the rich at disproportionately high rates, and then redistributing the tax proceeds—in the form of government benefits—disproportionately to the poor does bring Robin Hood to mind. So, if you are a fan of progressive taxation, you are probably a fan of Robin Hood.

CHAPTER XVII

What if You Actually Like This Stuff?

You never planned on that, did you? I'm sorry if I ruined your semester.

I assume that you're now taking the basic income tax course. That is the most logical tax course to take if you only take one tax course in law school. What if you decide to take a second course? Most people would opt for corporate income tax.

More than two? You might consider partnership tax. Many people consider partnership tax to be the most difficult tax subject. I know that sounds daunting, but look at it this way. Would you rather have to teach it to yourself, or would you rather have someone else (a professional teacher, no less) walk you through it? International tax courses are also lots of fun, and international tax knowledge can be quite lucrative, besides leading to some fun jobs in exotic locales.

Estate planning is a whole other way to go. That would include courses in the Federal Estate, Gift, and Generation-skipping taxes, and courses involving the taxation of trusts. The Federal Estate and Gift Taxes are far less important than they used to be, both in terms of how many people actually pay them, and what percentage of federal tax revenue they collect. But consider two things. First, a lot more people plan for them than pay them. Second, the people who worry about such taxes, no less pay them, are precisely the filthy rich people who make some of the best possible clients.

There are other fun tax classes. Tax policy courses, planning courses, and courses in Tax-Exempts come to mind. If you want to take many tax courses, see what is offered in your school, and, by all means, be sure to take the courses taught by the teachers who teach you well.

Then there is the (gulp) Tax LL.M. degree. It's still a buyers' market for law firms hiring associates, and many of them can afford not to bother even looking at an applicant for a tax practice position who doesn't have an LL.M. degree. Moreover, if you defer the LL.M. until after you are already in practice, you might be able to deduct many of your expenses. See Chapter VIII, Part D, on educational expenses.

To choose an LL.M. program, consult your tax teachers. For a handy guide to all of them, consider the TaxProf blog, taxprof. typepad.com.

Table of Cases